The Spirituality of Coziness

The Spirituality of Coziness

Experience Spiritual Growth through the Energy of Coziness for more Happiness, Contentment, and Satisfaction in Your Home, Relationships, and within Your Spiritual Self

MELISSA ALVAREZ

Published by

Adrema Press

The Spirituality of Coziness: Experience Spiritual Growth through the Energy of Coziness for more Happiness, Contentment, and Satisfaction in Your Home, Relationships, and within Your Spiritual Self © 2018, 2023 by Melissa Alvarez. All rights reserved. No part of this book may be used or reproduced in any manner whatsoever, including Internet usage, except in the case of brief quotations embodied in critical articles and reviews.

New Expanded and Revised Edition published by Adrema Press 2023

Originally Published in 2018 as *The Simplicity of Cozy* by Llewellyn Worldwide Ltd

ISBN: 978-1-59611-142-4

Cover Design by Melissa Alvarez

Any Internet references are current at the time of publication. The publisher cannot guarantee that a specific URL location will continue to be maintained.

OTHER BOOKS BY MELISSA ALVAREZ

365 Ways to Raise Your Frequency
365 Days to Raise Your Frequency Journal
Llewellyn's Little Book of Spirit Animals
Earth Frequency
Your Psychic Self
My Psychic Journal
Frequency By The Numbers
Animal Frequency
Animal Frequency Oracle Cards
Believe and Receive
Believe and Receive Mini Meditation Cards
Simply Give Thanks
Simply Give Thanks Gratitude Journal
Chakra Divination Card & Charts Activity Book
Chakra Divination Ultimate Balance Journal
The Essential Guide to Chakra Divination
Chakra Divination Card Deck
The Phoenix's Guide to Self-Renewal
Your Color Power
Analyze Your Handwriting
Ghosts, A Spirit Guide and A Past Life
Paranormal Investigative Groups Around the World

WRITING AS ARIANA DUPRE

Night Visions
Talgorian Prophecy
Talgorian Dragon
Briar Mountain
Paradise Designs
Paranormal Adventures

And much more...
Please Visit http://MelissaA.com for the complete booklist.

About the Author

Melissa Alvarez is a bestselling author, editor, and book cover designer who has written thirty-two books, novels, short stories, and mind/body/spirit nonfiction titles as well as nearly 500 articles on self-help, spirituality, and wellness. As a professional intuitive coach, energy worker, spiritual advisor, medium, and animal communicator with over 35 years of experience, Melissa has helped thousands of people bring clarity, joy, and balance into their lives. Melissa teaches others how to connect with their own intuitive nature and how to work with frequency for spiritual growth. She has appeared on number radio shows as both a guest and host. Melissa is the author of *365 Ways to Raise Your Frequency*, *Your Psychic Self*, *Animal Frequency*, *Earth Frequency*, *Llewellyn's Little Book of Spirit Animals*, *The Spirituality of Coziness*, *Simply Give Thanks* and many other titles. Her books with Llewellyn have been translated into multiple languages worldwide including Romanian, Russian, Chinese, French, Czech and Spanish. Please visit her website for a full list of her current titles.

Find Melissa Online at:
https://MelissaA.com
https://www.facebook.com/melissaalvarezauthor (main profile)
https://www.facebook.com/IamMelissaAlvarez (author page)

Other websites:
https://BookCovers.us
https://ThornRidge.com Online retail store
http://TopHatFriesians.com Barock Pinto & Friesian horses

DEDICATION

This book is dedicated to my husband, Jorge, who always brought so much coziness, warmth, and love to my life. I miss you every minute of every day. I'll love you forever and always.

CONTENTS

List of Try It Now Exercises   xv
Acknowledgments   xvii
Disclaimer   xix
Introduction   1

Chapter One: Cozy Cultural Ideals From Around the World

Hygge (Danish) Definition, History, Danish Roots   5
How to Recognize Hygge   7
Spiritual Growth through Hygge   9
Similar Cultural Concepts of Cozy: 12
    Fika (Sweden)   12
    Friluftsliv (Norway)   13
    Gemütlichkeit (German)   14
    Gezelligherd (Dutch)   15
    Koselig (Norway)   16
    Mys (Sweden)   17
Try It Now Exercise – Slow Down with Hygge   18
Cozy-adjacent: Additional Cultural Concepts for Wellness   20
    Jugaad (India)   20
    Kaizen (Japan)   21
    Lagom (Sweden)   22
    Shinrin-yoku (Japan)   24
    Sisu (Finland)   25
    Uitwaaien (Dutch)   26
    Wabi-Sabi (Japan)   27
The Soul Connection of Coziness in any Culture   28
Try It Now Exercise – Connect with your Core Spiritual Self through Coziness   31

Chapter Two: Create Coziness for Deeper Meaning

Getting Cozy for Comfort   33
Togetherness, Warmth, Lovingness, Inclusion   35
Light up Your Life   37
Creating a Cozy Home   40
Try it Now: Create A Cozy Room in Your Home   41
Coziness in Relationships   43
Can You Bring Coziness to Work?   45
Cozy Amid the Crazy   47
The Energy of Coziness   49
Get Cozy to Expand Your Consciousness   51
Try it Now: Create a Personal Sanctuary   53

Chapter Three: Making Cozy Personal

A Conversation with Your Higher Self   57
You Are Significant   59
Self-Care of Mind, Body, and Spirit   61
Ways to Appreciate Yourself More   63
Work/Life Balance   65
Try It Now Exercise – Take a *Me* Day   67
Creativity   68
Practice the Positive   70
Routines, Rituals, Normalcy, Knowing What to Expect   72
Peacefulness in Solitude   73
It's Okay to Say No   75
Try It Now Exercise – Soak in a Tub with Candles   76

Chapter Four: Embrace the Moments of Your Life

Meaningful Moments   79
Awareness of Being in the Now   81
Embracing Silence   83
Embracing Honesty   84

Simplify and Slow Down   85
Try It Now Exercise – Sit Quietly and Watch   87
Leave Technology Behind   88
Social Media   90
Try It Now Exercise – Go Tech-free for a Week   92
Living In the Moment   93
Examine the Little Things   95
Minimalistic Approach   97
Clutter can Hold You Back   99
Releasing What No Longer Serves You   100
Today is Tomorrow's Yesterday   102
Impulsive Behavior   104
The Frequency of a Moment   106
Try It Now Exercise – What Can You Release Today?   108

Chapter Five: Become More Mindful

What is Mindfulness?   111
The Energy of Self-Awareness   113
Mindfulness and Personal Growth   115
Develop a Calm Concentration   117
Being Reflective to Bring about Change   119
Finding Balance in Your Spirituality   121
Try It Now Exercise – A Working Meditation   122
Create Meaningful Relationships though Mindfulness   124
Pause and Reflect to Change Directions   126
Try It Now Exercise - Make a *Moving Toward Cozy* Project   128
Overcoming Obstacles to Mindfulness   129
Letting Your Mind Wander   131
Attention to Details   133
Mindfulness is Nonjudgmental   134
Making Mindfulness a Priority   136
Try It Now Exercise – Journaling/Coloring   138

Chapter Six: Spend Time in the Natural World

Connect with Nature   141
Rainy Days   143
Gardening for the Mind, Body, and Spirit   145
Bringing the Outside In   147
The Energy of the Natural World   149
Try It Now Exercise – Just Breathe   151
Spiritual Growth through Nature   153
The Allure of Being In the Forest   155
Try It Now Exercise – Create a Plant Sanctuary   157
The Spirit of Animals   159
Pick a Power Place   161
Frequency of Seasons for Spiritual Growth   163
Try It Now Exercise – Take a Hike or Go Camping   165

Chapter Seven: Emotional Coziness

Change Your Attitude   169
Empower the Self-Sabotaging You   171
Gratitude and Thankfulness   173
Working Your Way through Frustration   175
Finding Forgiveness   177
Seek Out the Sacred   179
Generosity   181
Try It Now Exercise – Give When It's Not Expected   183
Release Resentment   185
Feeling Entitled or Too Proud   187
Finding Success in Failures   189
Realistic and Unrealistic Expectations   191
Reflect and Plan   193
Try It Now Exercise – Make an Expectations List   195

Chapter Eight: Improve Your Spiritual Wellness

Yoga   197
Reiki   199
Dance   201
Travel   203
Focused Meditation   205
Try It Now Exercise – Guided Wellness Meditation   207
Express Yourself   209
Volunteer   211
Appreciate the Arts   213
Try It Now Exercise – Overall Wellness Checklist   215

Chapter Nine: The Transformational Energy of Spiritual Coziness

The Frequency of Letting Go   219
Subtle Energy Shifts   221
Communication Remedies   223
Look for New Fun   225
Power Up Your Spirit   227
Good Actions   230
Try It Now Exercise – Letting Go to Embrace Coziness   232
Make Your Own Miracles   233
Spontaneity   235
Busyness vs Restfulness   237
Put A Spring In Your Step   239
Your Values and Beliefs   241
Your Soul Journey Frequency   243
The Universal Cozy Connection   245
Try It Now Exercise – Coziness Transformational Challenge 247

Conclusion   249
Bibliography   251

LIST OF TRY IT NOW EXERCISES

Chapter One
Slow Down with Hygge   18
Connect with Your Core Spiritual Self through Coziness   31

Chapter Two
Create a Cozy Room in Your Home   41
Create a Personal Sanctuary   53

Chapter Three
Take a *Me* Day   67
Soak in a Tub with Candles   76

Chapter Four
Sit Quietly and Watch   87
Go Tech-Free for a Week   92
What Can You Release Today?   108

Chapter Five
A Working Meditation   122
Make a Moving Toward Cozy Project   128
Journaling / Coloring   138

Chapter Six
Just Breathe   151
Create A Plant Sanctuary   157
Take a Hike or Go Camping   165

Chapter Seven
Give When It's Not Expected   183
Make an Expectations List   195

List of Try It Now Exercises

Chapter Eight
Guided Wellness Meditation   207
Overall Wellness Checklist   215

Chapter Nine
Letting Go to Embrace Coziness   232
Coziness Transformational Challenge   247

ACKNOWLEDGEMENTS

I wouldn't be able to write without the support I have here at home. As always, thanks go out to my family, for understanding that earplugs are sometimes my best friends and that quick, easy-to-make dinners will suffice when deadlines are fast approaching.

To my parents, for their belief in me and checking to see how the book is coming along.

I have to give a very special thanks to my readers for your support. I write to teach others as we walk this pathway together and your feedback, questions, and correspondence is what keeps me writing more. Thank you!

DISCLAIMER

Please note that the information in this book is not meant to diagnose, treat, prescribe, or substitute consultation with a licensed medical or psychological professional. Both the author and the publisher recommend that you consult a medical practitioner before attempting the techniques outlined in this book.

Introduction

Life is a journey of lessons that ultimately leads to the growth of your soul. On this path, we all have different roles to carry out and lessons to learn. In this lifetime, on my path, one of my roles is to be a teacher of all things spiritual—to help others learn to connect to the intrinsic part of their essence that makes them who they are in spirit and to help them see and understand more than what can be seen with the eyes.

I've worked with vibrational energy, the frequency of being, for a long time, even before it was called *frequency*. I've taught others to experience energy connections in everything they do, how to understand and feel their own frequency, and how to raise their frequency and connect it with the frequency of others, of animals, of places, and of situations. *The Spirituality of Coziness* was born because of the frequency connection with the day-to-day situations that we find ourselves in—the idea that we can connect to the energy of even the simplest moments in our lives and allow that energy to affect us so we move forward and grow in positive and empowering ways. The book is designed to allow you to create tremendous positivity for yourself by becoming more aware of your ability to implement a sense of coziness to all you do,

Introduction

including the way you think and your approach to your spiritual path.

The Spirituality of Coziness is about feeling coziness while recognizing your soul essence through the connection you make to the Divine and to universal consciousness. It is meant to be a resource you can turn to time and time again, especially when you feel off-kilter. It is my hope that *The Spirituality of Coziness* will help guide you back on track during times of unbalance and that my words can enlighten you and bring you the focus needed to embrace the simple, cozy, everyday moments of your life. The increased awareness that a cozy feeling brings can help you rise above problems, if only for a moment, to appreciate the positive in your life. You can become a beacon of light not only within yourself but also to those around you.

Coziness is a way of life for many people around the world. It is a frequency connection at a very personal level that can bring about miraculous transformations at your core spiritual essence. When you make a shift in your energy to one of awareness of the little things, of a simple life where you are more connected to the moments that your essential self needs for growth, it leads to more joy and happiness. All parts of your general lifestyle are a part of and affect the coziness you experience on a daily basis. It's time to make a new and warm frequency connection within your lifestyle. Living the cozy life is a gift you give to yourself.

Embracing coziness isn't always as easy as just thinking happy thoughts or choosing the positive. Sure, *sometimes* it can be that easy, but often it requires you to actively choose and be consciously aware that you *are* choosing to add more coziness to your lifestyle. It is a feeling deep within your core spiritual being of understanding yourself and the choices you make at a soul level. It's all about making choices...and the choices are yours to make. Coziness, spirituality, and consciousness are all connected to the cosmos of Divine knowledge, all of which identify you as a spiritual being at your purest essence.

Feeling the charm of coziness can fill you with transformative energy. The simple act of becoming more sensitive to the cozy possibilities can turn your life from one filled with stress to one where you're more relaxed and happy. It doesn't happen in the blink of an eye, but as you become more aware you will be transformed. If you like to journal, write down things as you become aware of them so you can refer back to them in the future. Coziness will give you a sense of peace within and a greater understanding of the world around you.

You're always learning and growing on a spiritual level. You learn from your mistakes, grow on your path of self-discovery, and embody all that you are as a spiritual being. Embracing the frequency connection of coziness is recognizing the truth within your soul, living that truth, and appreciating yourself and those around you through your daily experiences.

Love, selflessness, joy, caring, and compassion are all keys to cozy living. When you put these keys into the locks of your life, you open yourself to the wonders the universe has to offer on every level. Now is the time to become one with your Divine Self, to open the doors of your mysteries and be thankful every step of the way. You hold these keys in your hands. It's up to you whether you use them to empower your own soul essence or whether you allow them to sit idly by. It is your choice to be

Introduction

aware of the cozy things in your life that bring more enlightenment.

For those who have learned to open to awareness, to be in the moment, and embrace coziness, it often becomes a way of life. It is so interwoven into their being that it happens without conscious thought. It is part of who they are, how they behave, and how they interact with others. The Danish are a prime example of this, and we'll discuss their concept of coziness called hygge in chapter one.

It is my hope that *The Spirituality of Coziness* will enable you to make more soulful connections to the moments of your life and to find appreciation in all you are and in all you experience. This book is written as a beginner's guide and is filled with exercises that will help you enhance the spirituality of coziness in your life as you grow on your spiritual path.

I invite you to join me as I guide you along this journey. I also invite you to participate in the Coziness Transformational Challenge. This is a thirty-day (or more) challenge that you can do whenever you feel ready to start. It will help you change your thought patterns and redirect your actions in ways that will change your life to embrace coziness and bring about more joy and happiness while you enjoy the moments of your life. You'll find details about the challenge at the end of the book, so keep it in mind as you read (or check it out before you start reading). It's going to be fun so let's do this!

Chapter One
COZY CULTURAL IDEALS FROM AROUND THE WORLD

What does living a cozy life mean to you? To me it means a warmth within my home, within my being and between my family and friends. It is a close feeling of happiness and joy. In this chapter, I want to introduce you to some of the different cultural practices from around the world that bring about a feeling of contentment with life. To start, let's focus on the Danish practice of hygge.

HYGGE (DANISH) DEFINATION, HISTORY, DANISH ROOTS

Hygge (pronounced HUE-guh) is used as a descriptive term in the Danish culture that reflects the Danish lifestyle. Because it describes various qualities of their way of life, it doesn't have one specific definition. The term *hygge* originated in Norway during the sixteenth century, where it first appeared in some Danish writings. It comes from the Norwegian term *hygga* which means "to comfort."

Chapter One

If you wanted to explain hygge to someone, a good description would be that it is a Danish custom of finding pleasure in the simple things, of making the ordinary extraordinary, of adding more meaningfulness to every aspect of your day, and to make each moment special by actually being *present* in that moment. It is a feeling of well-being that gives those who practice hygge a cozy feeling of deep satisfaction and contentment. It is the celebration of warmth, companionship, respect for others, family, and grace. It is an increased awareness of your inner self, the people, and the world around you. It is creating an enjoyable atmosphere that feels safe, comfortable, and emotionally warm. Experiencing hygge enriches your life and brings you more happiness through the celebration of the ordinary, everyday moments that are often overlooked during the hustle and bustle of a busy day.

In Scandinavian countries, especially in winter, there is less daylight and it can be bitterly cold. In some areas, the temperature can be as low as -50 degrees Fahrenheit. If you've ever been stuck inside during a snowstorm, or any other type of bad weather, then you know it's easy to get cabin fever but if it is 50 degrees below zero outside, then the warmth of a fire, a hot cup of coffee or tea, and the coziness of home is much more desirable. The practice of hygge is thought to have come about to bring more warmth, light, and happiness during the cold, dark winters so that being stuck inside became more bearable. It helped to alleviate any feelings of sadness or depression by replacing them with feelings of coziness, warmth, and the appreciation of a simple life through a positive state of mind. In other words, it helped people get through difficult winters.

Over time, the practice of hygge expanded to all seasons and at any time during the day or night. It is still a preferred practice during the darkness of winter, when it's easier to obtain a feeling of warm coziness as a cold, windy, winter storm is happening outside.

Hygge takes people back to times when things were simple, back to the good old days when there was less stress, more companionship, and more understanding. When the world wasn't easily accessible through the Internet, and you had to think of ways to enjoy your life without relying on technology, computers, or smartphones. It's based in making your environment welcoming, warm, and hospitable. Connecting with others is also the basis of hygge. In the past, it was the telling of stories while sitting around the fire having refreshments. When you remember times like these, it gives you a bond to the coziness of hygge and the creation of an aspect of culture. You don't have to be Danish to experience hygge. You can find peace, contentment, and enjoyment of the little things, the special moments, wherever you live in the world.

How to Recognize Hygge

How do you know when you're experiencing hygge? In the beginning, it may be a little difficult to determine what is hygge and what isn't, but with a little practice you'll be able to recognize hygge immediately. One thing is certain though—you can't buy hygge in any store or from any person. It has to be experienced.

Hygge is a feeling. You can also think of it as an emotion, mood, or state of mind. When you're experiencing hygge you

Chapter One

feel safe, warm, and cozy. Hygge brings about a sense of empowerment because you feel the truth of the moment at a soul level. Hygge can bring all parts of your being together in one moment. You may physically be in an environment that you find appealing; you may be emotionally satisfied, and mentally relaxed.

Let's say you're in a restaurant with cozy lighting at an intimate booth where you aren't really aware of all of the other people around you, and you're dining alone because you were bombarded by people all day at work and need some downtime by yourself. This is a good time to mentally relax and let go of any emotional stress you've been feeling. As you wait for your meal, you sip whatever you've chosen to drink and let the day melt away from your mind, body, and spirit. You feel connected to the joy and happiness of simply being. Now let's say you tell a friend about your dinner alone and how it gave you time to think, released the negatives and embraced the positives, and recharged you. Because you told your friend, and they see a calm relaxation in your eyes that wasn't there yesterday, now they may want to try the same thing so they can feel the same calmness. They want to experience hygge too. This is how it spread from Denmark throughout the world. People visited Denmark and experienced it firsthand, then took that experience back home with them in their hearts and recreated it in their homes and lives. Hygge is warm and inviting lighting, spending time with those you love enjoying the simple pleasures in life, good food, good drinks, warmth, and togetherness. It is wrapping up in a blanket and snuggling into the corner of your couch with a good book and a fire crackling in the fireplace.

You'll know that you're experiencing a hygge moment because suddenly you'll feel completely in the *now* of that moment. You'll have a heightened sense of awareness of what is happening and the people around you. Sometimes it might feel as if time is in slow motion and you focus on only one thing even though a lot is going on. It's an *aha* moment where everything clicks together and makes complete sense. You'll feel as if you're wrapped in a blanket of appreciation, comfort, and joy. It can be a bit overwhelming at times and make you sit back and simply think wow.

When you've experienced that deep cozy feeling of hygge, you'll seek it out because it calls to you on a soul level. You'll probably start creating your own moments of hygge instead of waiting for it to come to you. When you create it, you can encompass everything you desire in that moment or during an event and share what hygge means to you with others.

Spiritual Growth through Hygge

As the guardian of your individual path and purpose, you are responsible for learning and achieving the lessons you set forth for yourself. You are responsible for your own path; you have free will to improve your spiritual essence through the earthly experience. The growth, or non-growth, that you create here is what you'll take with you, on a soul level, when you return home.

Purposefully creating hygge in your life and looking for naturally occurring hygge moments will help make your journey easier and will allow your soul to experience spiritual growth. It's when you get too caught up in the physical, in obtaining the material, and neglect soul growth that you can

Chapter One

walk a difficult path. Now that doesn't mean you'll never experiences difficulties—you will because some lessons chosen prior to birth are hard—but it *does* mean that focusing on soul growth while experiencing hygge creates feelings of peacefulness, calmness, and thankfulness.

Any growth, increased awareness, and balance you experience during this lifetime will become a permanent, eternal part of you. Experiencing hygge enables you to cherish your soul by immersing yourself in your daily adventures. Nurturing hygge feelings is like shining a flashlight down a dark path, bringing to light all that is unseen so you may walk an illuminated path unafraid and with a sense of calm wonderment.

As you take a look at yourself, do you see a need for more hygge in your life? Can you make improvements by changing your attitude so you're reducing your stress and finding simpler, more grounded approaches to the situations you encounter? If so, then make internal changes by changing your thought patterns first and your actions second. Can you let go of a need for constant perfection and any insecurities you may be holding on to and simply enjoy being yourself? By working within first, you're working with your subconscious mind and your soul connection, which will bring about changes in your physical world because of your new thought patterns and beliefs.

Being aware of the hygge surrounding the change will strengthen it even further. Be sincere in your desires, and wondrous blessings will result. If you're not sure where to start, maybe just sitting in a quiet, dimly lit room, staring into the flickering flame of a candle can help you begin or you could play a fireplace video on your television if you don't have access to a real one. Ponder where you've been and where you want to go. Plan different hygge situations that will create opportunities for spiritual growth. Maybe you could host a hygge function with friends or join different groups online that practice hygge or maybe you can find hygge events in your neighborhood to attend. At the midpoint of this chapter, there's an exercise to help you slow down with hygge.

Hygge enhances all we are and all we do. It means accepting things and finding delight in life instead of wishing for something else. Overlooking hygge moments are missed opportunities to connect to the true nature of ourselves.

Every day become aware of the hygge around you. Maybe it's the scent of the fresh fallen rain, or the chirp of a bird outside your window, or sipping coffee with your friend. The other day I was deep in thought pumping gas because I was worried about one of our dogs that wasn't eating. I must have looked worried because the man beside me, who I hadn't even noticed, said to me out of the blue "I hope you have a wonderful day today." I looked at him, smiled, thanked him and wished the same for him. This is an example of a hygge moment. He didn't have to say a word to me. That small nicety from him seemed to say that everything would be okay. I got a special food for my dog at the clinic and when I offered it to her, she gobbled it right down.

You can find the coziness of hygge all around you. The more you notice it, experience it, and use it to grow spiritually, the better your life will be. You will feel more positivity even if there is a ton of snow outside. Look for ways to enhance your spirit with hygge.

Chapter One

SIMILAR CULTURAL CONCEPTS OF COZY

The concept of coziness is seen in many cultures. Let's take a brief look at some cultural concepts that are similar to hygge. Like hygge, some of the terms are difficult to translate into English because they mean multiple things or are more of a descriptive term rather than a straightforward definition.

Fika (Sweden)

In Sweden, there is a tradition called *fika* (pronounced fee-kah), also known as the Swedish coffee break. It is a core part of the Swedish lifestyle that includes snacks, drinks, and feeling content. In Sweden, you can experience fika around every corner. It's a time to slow down, to relax, and to enjoy quiet time with yourself or cheerfulness with other people. Fika means hanging out, talking, catching up, or making plans, all while having refreshments. You can also experience fika by yourself whenever you take a break. Fika was created around the Swedish thought that you shouldn't work any longer than you absolutely have to work. And then, you take a break. You might go back to the work or you might be finished for the day, but taking fika breaks throughout the day is necessary in the Swedish culture. Fika means taking things in moderation and making time for family and friends. Like hygge, it's all about slowing down and enjoying the good things and special moments of life, except fika is about a particular moment.

Where can you experience fika? Pretty much anywhere. Any time you take a break from what you're doing to have a cup of coffee or tea and a baked snack is time for fika. You might be at work, at home, out shopping, at a park, or attending an event. Fika can happen anywhere and at any time of day or night. You can also plan to meet your friends after work at the local coffee shop or café to spend some time together. That's fika.

Friluftsliv (Norway)
Whether you go cross-country skiing, dog sledding, or running, or you simply take a walk, you're participating in what Norwegians call *friluftsliv* (pronounced free-luufts-leav). It is being in the great outdoors and connecting with nature. The term friluftsliv means *free air life*. To Norwegians, it's much more than just being outside. It means that being present in nature is good for the mind, body, and spirit. When you participate in friluftsliv, you experience a sense of spiritual wellness, a heightened level of consciousness, and a deeper connection to your own spiritual self.

Breathing in the fresh air, feeling grounded as you walk across the land, and feeling as if you're part of something bigger than just your physical body is all part of friluftsliv. It is a lifestyle of becoming one with nature to increase your own wholeness of spirit. Getting away from the stress of your work week by being outside and appreciating the world around you is relaxing to your mind, energizing to your physical body, and rejuvenating to your core soul essence.

In Norway, friluftsliv is a lifestyle that is taught to children when they are young and continues throughout a lifetime. There are many ways you can experience friluftsliv even if you don't live in Norway. Anytime that you go outside you are embracing the experience of being part of nature, whether you're gardening, meditating, camping, hiking, walking, running, or taking pictures of your surroundings. There are

Chapter One

many ways you can experience friluftsliv alone or with family or friends. Maybe you decide to make sandcastles at the beach and are aware of the feeling of the grains of sand, the sound of the water lapping against the shore, and the sun on your skin. Friluftsliv relaxes you and gives you a sense of coziness by being part of nature.

Gemütlichkeit (German)

The Germany concept of *gemütlichkeit* (pronounced guh-MYOOT-lik-kyt) is used to describe a feeling of warm, cozy, companionship. Gemütlichkeit differs from hygge in that it also means to have increased productivity or to be profitable in business. You'll often hear this word used more during the winter months because, like hygge, it describes the way the Germans create atmosphere within their homes, work environments, and during social events—especially when it's cold outside. Gemütlichkeit differs from hygge in that it also means to have increased productivity or to be profitable in business. Some believe that the concept of hygge actually originated from the German word gemütlichkeit and was originally a German cultural concept that worked its way into the Danish culture.

If you're lingering after a meal just to hang out and enjoy the company of the people you're with while experiencing good cheer, happy times, and friendliness, that's gemütlichkeit. It is playing classical music and drinking tea while spending times with friends or loved ones. It is feeling a safe peace of mind while enjoying quality time in the company of others.

Gemütlichkeit means to give your undivided attention to those around you. It can also be experienced when you participate in your favorite activities, whether it's some type of sport or simply reading a good book. The lighting of a room is also important to obtain gemütlichkeit—dim and warm makes a room look more inviting. Lots of candles add more presence and a sense of coziness, which is perfect for creating this environment. If it's a holiday, then the decorations associated with that holiday can add to the feeling. Beautiful presentations of food, snacks, and decorations in addition to the lighting can truly add a wonderful sense of gemütlichkeit to your next get-together.

Gezelligheid (Dutch)

Gezelligheid (pronounced geh-zel-lyg-hide) is a term that is difficult to translate. It can mean socializing with friends, having fun with loved ones, togetherness, or being friendly to strangers. It goes beyond simply being in a cozy atmosphere, although that is part of gezelligheid, and can mean relaxing, getting comfortable, enjoyment, and being extroverted and outgoing. For the Dutch, it means to get out and about to spend time in old-fashioned shops, boutiques, or a brown café.

Feelings of warmth, companionship, happiness, and love for family and friends are central to gezelligheid. It is snuggling up with your significant other to watch a movie with a warm cozy blanket. Going to a music concert where you sit on the lawn is also gezelligheid. It is going with friends for a night out that includes dinner at a nice restaurant, a movie, and then stopping by a local establishment for tea, coffee, or drinks.

Gezelligheid is a lifestyle that is lived year-round. In the summer, it means doing lots of outdoor activities like going to the beach, camping, watching the sunrise or sunset, going out

Chapter One

on a boat, or having a picnic. In the winter, gezelligheid is brought indoors with warm cozy lighting, especially candlelight or small lamps that give off a warm glow instead of bright, florescent lighting. It is gathering around the dinner table for a holiday feast.

You can practice a gezelligheid lifestyle in any location, implementing social coziness into your life and taking it with you wherever you go.

Koselig (Norway)

When you think of warm and fuzzy coziness in every aspect of daily living, think of the Norwegian word *koselig* (pronounced KOOS-uh-lee). Koselig is similar to hygge in that it means to use warm lighting in your home, have friends over, and to experience happiness and joy through togetherness. However, in Norway, *koselig* is a term that is applied to everything from your kitchen dishes to the sweater you're wearing or what you plan to do on the weekend.

Koselig is vaguely translated as cozy, but it is coziness without borders. It surpasses winter and goes into summer. It can't contain itself within your house or work environment. It is anywhere and everywhere, you just have to know how to look for it, how to experience it, and how to create it for yourself. Koselig is a way to seize the moments of friendship, comfort, trust, happiness, joy, togetherness, and even quiet, reflective times. One word encompasses it all and is applicable to everything from a person, a conversation, or the atmosphere of a place. It's important in Norway to take advantage of good weather because it can change unexpectedly, but they don't complain about the snow either. Norwegians have a positive mind-set, which helps them get through the roughest of winters.

Some of the ways you can create koselig in your life, even if you live in a tropical climate, is to develop an appreciation for everything and everyone around you. When you can look at the details, notice the small things in life, and feel the warmth, happiness, and joy that the thing or person brings into your life, then you're practicing koselig.

Mys (Sweden)

In addition to the Swedish coffee break, the people of Sweden also have another concept of coziness called *mys* (pronounced mee-s) that is practiced year-round. Mys means to intentionally create comfort and coziness in your home, similar to hygge. For example, Fredagsmys or Cozy Friday, is the celebration of mys every Friday to relax and create some downtime after a hectic week at work. In Sweden, it is celebrated with junk food galore (especially chips), candles, warm blankets, pajamas, pizza, soda, wine and beer, along with a movie or watching television as a family until you fall asleep on the couch. Singles may have a similar get-together with friends at someone's home to do the same sort of things for Fredagsmys.

While not all Swedish people participate in Fredagsmys, most do enjoy mys by creating a cozy living environment, by being increasingly more mindful, and by having an awareness of being in the moment. They savor the warmth of mys during special occasions, holidays, or even for no reason other than to connect to their own sense of quiet calm and inner joy.

Chapter One

Practicing mys means that it is completely fine, and expected, for you to have a lazy night all cuddled up in front of the television with a snack. It keeps you calm when you start to feel locked down and bored. It's finding joy through the simple pleasures in life like reading a book. Mys means it's okay to slow things down to almost a halt, to embrace a slower and simpler lifestyle. To be okay with not rushing to and fro in a hectic blur but instead to sit calmly and peacefully, enjoying the mys of the moment, the people you're with, and the atmosphere you've created.

Try It Now Exercise:
SLOW DOWN WITH HYGGE

Hygge can be practiced at any time and for any reason. Life can sometimes get very hectic and, when it does, you might feel like you're running full steam ahead with no end in sight. This can lead to stress, anxiety, or feeling completely overwhelmed. If you find yourself in this type of situation, then it's time to have a hygge experience, to look for the simple things, to get cozy and first take some time for yourself, and then spend some quality time with friends and family.

For this exercise let's start with you. Let's say you've just gotten off work and it's been a difficult day. On your way home stop and pick up food from your favorite restaurant so you don't have to cook. Instead of calling it in ahead of time, wait until you get there to order the food. While you wait, have something to drink and maybe an appetizer. Imagine letting go of all of the stress that's accumulated within you. Pay attention to the moments happening around you. Look at the people around you; notice their moods and what they're doing. Do you see any awe-inspiring moments between people? If so, think about how seeing their interactions make you feel. As you sit there, purposefully imagine the positivity of white light moving through your frequency, your own personal vibration, the energy of all that you are. Imagine it removing any negativity that has gotten stuck in your energy. Imagine the white light flowing out of you, either through the top of your head, the bottoms of your feet, or out the tips of your fingers, taking any negativity with it, leaving you feeling relaxed, grounded, and stress free. When the to-go order is ready and you're on the way home, keep this positive, relaxed feeling within you.

Once you're at home, put on some of your favorite music at a low volume. Change out of your work clothes into something comfortable. Plan to have a movie night with your family or friends and include your favorite snacks and drinks. After dinner, turn off all the lights and enjoy the movie with those you love. Or, if you prefer to skip the movie, get out some board games or cards and have fun playing them together. Turn on lamps instead of the overhead lights to create a cozy atmosphere.

Choose your preferred entertainment. The point is to have a cozy, relaxing evening with people you're close to. While I've given you a sample exercise, you can also create a night of hygge for yourself in the same way to feel stress free and happy as you connect to its spirit.

If you're not in the mood for company, you might choose to take a long, hot shower or soak in the tub and then get into your pajamas. Select a good book, snuggle up on the couch or

Chapter One

in bed, and immerse yourself in the story. Stay up as late as you want or go to bed early to catch up on your sleep.

You can create a night of hygge for yourself anytime by creating a warm, cozy environment, having some of your favorite foods and drinks, relaxing and enjoying activities either alone or with family or friends, to feel stress free and happy as you connect to the energy of hygge.

Cozy-Adjacent: Additional Cultural Concepts for Wellness

In this section, I want to introduce you to some cozy-adjacent ideas. These are cultural concepts and practices you can use to add an additional layer of coziness to your life. They are different and unique. They deal with repairs, business, doing everything in moderation, forest bathing, walking in the wind, and finding beauty in imperfections. Check them out and decide if you'd like to implement some of these practices in your life.

Jugaad (India)

If you've ever had to come up with a creative way to repair something, even if it's only for the short term, you've participated in a cultural concept called *jugaad* (pronounced dzu-GAHD). In Hindi, the word *jugaad* means "an ingenious fix." It is often a frugal repair, like using tape to temporarily cover a hole or to hold something in place. It's a way to get by with less, to make do with what you already have, and to figure out a way to do something that is creative and innovative.

While fixing things doesn't seem like a cozy activity at first, it can be. If you gather up things that need repair around the house and get everyone in the family to participate in doing those repairs, then it can be a fun and cozy way to spend time together. Play to each person's strengths when assigning the repair jobs so it's fun instead of a chore. Work together and get creative. It will give you a sense of accomplishment when the job is done. Add some snacks and drinks and put on music at a low volume in the background and you've just created a hygge environment around your jugaad event.

If you've ever watched a secret agent movie, you've seen the character come up with unique solutions or create gadgets from ordinary things that will get them out of danger. That's the heart of jugaad. You can also find jugaad in the business world where corporations look for ingenuity and creativity in coming up with new ways to solve daily problems. Jugaad can often lead to wonderful new inventions when approached from the perspective of frugality and innovation.

Kaizen (Japan)

There is a Japanese concept called *kaizen* (pronounced keye-ZEN), which is primarily used in business, that means to practice continuous improvement in the workplace. Kaizen means that all employees, regardless of their position within the company, are encouraged to submit any ideas they have that will help make the business run better. Usually these are just small improvements about things the employees encounter daily—for instance the way things are run in the lunchroom. Employees can share the idea whenever they get it instead of waiting to submit ideas monthly or during a yearly

Chapter One

evaluation. The ideas are then implemented by the company to see if they do indeed make things run more smoothly. This process is a fantastic idea because it makes employees feel as if their opinions matter and that they are a valued part of the company (which they are or kaizen wouldn't be in place) and when you have happy employees, the company runs much better overall.

The concept of kaizen can also be applied to your own life to bring about more happiness and positivity. The best way to use kaizen personally is to get organized and make small changes that will help you reach the overall goal. If you want to become more spiritually enlightened, then create a long-term plan that outlines the topics you want to learn about, then, as you learn about each one, keep a journal, daily planner, or calendar where you can note your daily progress (or weekly if you're short on time). You can also make notes on your phone or computer if you prefer to use technology over writing something down in a journal or notebook. Each change you make, each improvement, aids you in obtaining your goal of becoming more spiritually enlightened. You'll find that using kaizen in your personal life helps eliminate stumbling blocks, keeps your life running smoothly, and gives you a sense of well-being and overall happiness.

Lagom (Sweden)

The Swedish idea of *lagom* (pronounced LAH-gom) means being moderate in everything. The idea of lagom is often expressed as not too little, not too much, just right. When you practice lagom, it means that you should have a moderate personality (not too dull but not too flamboyant and outgoing), you should have middle-of-the-road point of views that don't take one side over the other, you should dress moderately (not dull and plain but not flashy or extravagant either) and you should have a good time but not too much fun. Lagom is about only taking or experiencing what you need—no more and no less. It is about having self-restraint, living simply, and being happy with what you have. Practicing lagom can help you lead a more balanced life.

Practicing lagom keeps arguments to a minimum and lends itself to helping people feel more contentment with their lives just as they are. When you practice lagom, there isn't a constant desire for more. You're quite content with what you have. If you do decide to go over the top at an event and dress a little on the extravagant side, like wearing a brightly patterned piece of clothing, or bring a gourmet dish, like shrimp and lobster instead of mashed potatoes or bread, because you're hoping for a reaction about how nice you look or what a great dish you brought, will probably be met with no response from others...as in not a mention, no reaction whatsoever. Why? Because it's not important to make a big deal over something that doesn't fit with the lagom ideal of being moderate. If it's not important, then just ignore it. Lagom is always positive, whether you're eliminating clutter, enjoying a lagom meal, creating a sense of space in your home, adding to your wardrobe, buying a new car, fixing something that has broken, planning a vacation, or pretty much anything you do in life. Lagom is doing the essential, necessary, things in life and knowing when you're about to cross the line into doing the unessential and stopping at that point.

Chapter One

Shinrin-Yoku (Japan)

In Japanese medicine, *shinrin-yoku* (pronounced shin-rihn-yo-koo) is crucial to both healing and preventive health care. It means "forest bathing," which in turn means if you spend time in the forest, you will lower your stress levels. Since stress can cause all kinds of illness, if the stress is eliminated your health will be better. Plants also produce phytoncides, which protects the plant from fungi, insects, and other types of bacteria. When people are exposed to plant phytoncides, it has a positive effect on our bodies. They can help us feel less stress, can lower blood pressure, or have other health benefits. Some plants produce more phytoncides than others (for example, an onion), and these types of plants are often used in aromatherapy and holistic medicine.

In order to obtain the most benefit from shinrin-yoku, you should enter the forest relaxed and in tune with your inner self. Practicing shinrin-yoku can help reduce your blood pressure, boost your immune system, have shorter recovery times when you're sick, elevate your mood, and help you focus. When you're in a forest, connecting with its energy, you can also experience an increase in your own intuition, obtain clarity of purpose, and connect with your higher self or your core spiritual essence. Shinrin-yoku is considered therapy for mind, body, and spirit through the connection with the earth and the plants and animals that live on Earth.

When you're practicing shinrin-yoku, it is more than just walking through the woods. If you take time to connect to the flow of energy of the forest by taking a few minutes to sit quietly on a rock or against a tree, then you can truly feel its life essence, which has a quieting and steadying effect that can help you heal, refocus, and gain purpose in your life.

Sisu (Finland)

The people of Finland have been practicing the idea of *sisu* (pronounced see-su) for hundreds of years. For the Finnish it is a cultural life philosophy that helps them endure impossibly difficult situations, it's what keeps them going through hard times, and what enables them to see bad situations through to a resolution.

Sisu is the Finnish art of courage—an attitude within us that enables us to persevere, to be resilient and stoic in our thoughts and actions. It is the reserve of power within us that fuels our spirit when we think we can't endure anything else. It is an unwavering determination when faced with adversity, it is incredible courage when we don't think we can be brave, it is jumping in with both feet even when the possibility of failure is great, it is having hope and faith that everything will work out okay even when everything suggests otherwise. Sisu means that within each person there is a well of strength that we don't even realize that we have but that we can call upon in the darkest of days to get us through.

When faced with challenging situations, whether they are physical, mental, or emotional, Sisu is the psychological competence that enables us to overcome and move forward. It means to have humility, honesty, and integrity during the tough times. In other words, it means to have the guts to do what needs to be done, even if we think we can't accomplish the tasks at hand.

Chapter One

Embracing Sisu can help you go beyond what you think you're capable of doing. It enables you to keep going with others may think you should quit; it is the will to succeed when others think you will fail. Sisu helps you to surpass what you think you can accomplish by enabling you to push yourself beyond your limits by connecting to your internal well of power, strength, and courage.

When you're one with the sisu energy within you, there is no doubt that you will succeed during difficult times. You press on, move forward, knowing without a doubt in your mind, body, and spirit, that you will endure any difficulties through determination, courage and your own inner strength, and in the end, you will be successful.

Uitwaaien (Dutch)

The Dutch concept of *uitwaaien* (pronounced out-vwy-ehn) means "to walk in the wind." It also means to get out into the country to clear your head, get some fresh air, and let go of anything that is worrying you. If you live in the city and all you can do is take a walk in the park, then do that. If there aren't any parks around, then you can still feel the wind as you walk down the sidewalk. The point is to get outside and connect to the energy of the wind.

Most times, uitwaaien is something you do alone, so you can connect to your core essence, find your balance as you consider what worries you, and decide how to release those worries and move forward in life. Sometimes you just need to take a break from other people and get outside to feel the wind on your face, the earth beneath your feet, and smell the scents of the natural world. This doesn't mean you can't experience uitwaaien if you're with someone else. If you're both quiet and reflective on the walk and individually experiencing uitwaaien, then it will work for both of you. It's harder to experience it with someone else if you're engaging in conversation, though.

If you live near a beach, there's nothing better than taking a walk in the sand and feeling the water lap at your toes as the wind blows against your body. You feel the dampness of the air and the salt sticking to your skin (and sometimes the sand) as the wind creates wondrous new hair styles for you. It is during this time that you can make important decisions, consider your life and where you want to go, or to connect with your own spirituality. While uitwaaien is a Dutch concept, it can be practiced anywhere and everywhere because wind is something we all can experience regardless of where we live.

Wabi-Sabi (Japan)

Not only is *wabi-sabi* (pronounced wah-bee-sah-bee) a fun word to say, it's also an excellent concept of appreciation that the Japanese embrace. Wabi-sabi means to celebrate the beauty in the imperfections of age and wear. A wooden chest may have chips or cracks so that it's not perfect, but then again, nothing ever is. It's those chips and cracks that give it character, that are representative of what the chest has been through since it was created, it is what makes it unique. Wabi-sabi can also be your favorite item of clothing that has tears or holes in it but you just can't throw away. Now this doesn't mean to see broken things as wabi-sabi when they're actually trash. It's being able to tell the difference and to appreciate the imperfections in worn things and the natural beauty that surrounds us. It is an appreciation of things that are handmade from natural materials instead of being perfectly made by a machine without flaws or any uniqueness.

Wabi-sabi means to embrace our life experiences that have given us scars, wrinkles, and other imperfections on our body. It is realizing that the inner changes you've made in your life are what makes you the person you are today. Wabi-sabi is acceptance of all things, yourself, and other people, with all of their defects, faults, and imperfections. Within imperfection, we can find the perfection of our souls. By appreciating the uniqueness of the old, it makes us less inclined to go out and buy the new, which leads to more attention to the details of what is currently in our lives. Practicing wabi-sabi means to be humble, appreciative, and to see the beauty within.

THE SOUL CONNECTION OF COZINESS IN ANY CULTURE

No matter the culture, when you think of coziness, you probably think of comfort, safety, atmosphere, and enjoying special times with friends and family. That being said, there are also soul connections associated with the forms of coziness in different countries around the world. In order to connect with the spirit of cozy, you first have to connect to the spirit of you.

Your soul connection is what makes you distinctively you. You will have shared interests with others during your life, but your own path is unique and special. Both our conscience and our conscious mind are part of our spiritual being. Before birth, we are in our spiritual body of energy and exist with our soul and our subconscious mind. After birth, we still have our soul and subconscious mind, which are the eternal parts of our being that we are never without, but now we also have a physical body and a physical mind that allows us to exist on the earthly plane in order to learn lessons that will allow us spiritual growth so that we may progress to higher spiritual realms.

As humans, our conscience is what guides us to do right instead of wrong and our conscious mind makes us pay attention and be more aware of the world around us instead of being oblivious to our surroundings. Because we are individual and different souls, this uniqueness of spirit is what allows one person to experience coziness in their home with warm lighting and allows someone else to experience a moment of coziness when they notice and focus on the hum of the air conditioner or heater during a meeting at work.

This special soul and frequency connection increases awareness, which is one of the core principles of experiencing a cozy situation in many cultures. We are guided by our inner voice, higher self, and spiritual being, all of which are parts of our soul essence. When we let our soul connection within ourselves guide us, it can help us see coziness in situations where we may not have noticed it before.

When you are aware of the coziness around you, then you can connect with it, appreciate it, and cherish the experience, which also allows you to better connect to the truth held within your divine soul. As you uncover your own truths, and nurture those truths, then you'll begin to experience even more coziness in your daily life. It's an awesome circle of acknowledgment, appreciation, discovery, and spiritual growth.

Chapter One

    Remember that hygge is about experiencing the little things, the niceties in life, as well as the big events. As you begin to live a cozy life, start your morning with a few moments of being thankful for your spiritual path, the people who love and care about you, the accomplishments you've made, and the things surrounding you. Then as you move throughout your day, when someone does something nice or unexpected for you, or any little thing that makes you feel joyful, take a moment to acknowledge and to appreciate the experience. The more you look for cozy moments, the sooner it will become an ingrained habit, a heightened awareness, and an integral part of your spiritual being.

    As you experience coziness along your individual soul path, always remember that you are a spiritual being and the truth of your soul is within you. It attunes you to the awareness of everything cozy. The more you strengthen your foundation in this lifetime, through responsibility and understanding of your spiritual journey, the closer your connection to your soul and the more often you'll have cozy moments. When the connection is close, then it's easier to progress in forward motion to attain the goals you've set for yourself in this lifetime.

Try It Now Exercise:
CONNECT WITH YOUR CORE SPIRITUAL SELF THROUGH COZINESS

Before you begin this meditation exercise, first create a cozy setting for yourself. A small nook area or a corner of a room will work for this purpose. This area is your cozy corner. Some of the things you may want to put in your cozy corner are:

1. A comfortable chair or big pillows to lean against if you're creating the space in an alcove or nook area.
2. A blanket that you can curl up inside of or throw over you.
3. A little table so you can place your drink on it.
4. If you can, put a few little potted plants in the area that will increase the cozy effect.
5. Make sure the lighting has a warm and cozy feeling as well. →You can use dim lighting in the corner of the room from a lamp or hang some string lights in the nook area.

Once your cozy corner is all set up, you're ready to begin working on connecting to your core spiritual self. Start by feeling the coziness you've created around you. If you're angry or upset prior to starting this exercise, then take deep breaths, with each inhale imagine pure positive energy flowing into you, with each exhale imagine all the negative energy leaving your body. Even if you're not feeling out of sorts, the breathing technique will help you get in balance, feel calm, and connect to the coziness you've created around you.

Now close your eyes. Imagine your spiritual body within your physical body. See the whirling spirals of energy that make up the chakras (the seven energy centers of spiritual power in the human body) within you. Follow the flow of this energy; feel the love within it as it moves through you. Now, imagine a swirling pathway that leads to your core spiritual self. Follow the energy to that place. You might see it as a room or as the blackness of space filled with stars. In this space, you see your spiritual energy. You may see yourself as a swirling beacon of light, filled with many beautiful colors, or you may see yourself in human form, glowing with white light.

Use creative visualization to imagine your core spiritual self in your cozy corner with you. Once you both are comfortable, start a conversation with your core spiritual self and ask if there are any important messages you should know at this time. Trust in any impressions you receive, anything you hear clairaudiently, and know you are in communication with your true soul essence. When you feel the conversation is at an end, follow the energy path back to the spirals of chakra energy within your physical body, then, when you feel reconnected to your physical self, open your eyes.

It's a good idea to write down the messages you received during this exercise so you can refer back to them as you move forward on your spiritual path. Any time you desire, you can repeat this exercise to obtain more knowledge about spirituality from your core spiritual being, to find the source and reasons for fear in your life, and to discover more about yourself on a spiritual level. Anything you need to know in this lifetime, you already know at your core spiritual essence. All you have to do is connect and ask for help in understanding.

Chapter Two

CREATE COZINESS FOR DEEPER MEANING

When you practice creating coziness in your life, you add a depth of meaning that you may not have experienced without it. Feeling happy and content with the way your life is going, with your job and the people in your life, enables you to move forward on your path. As you recognize the additional benefits coziness offers, you'll also realize that getting your cozy on is a great way to dig deeper into the meaning of your life.

GETTING COZY FOR COMFORT

Coziness is all about being comfortable. When you are comfortable, you have a warm feeling inside and everything is right within your world. There are several ways to enjoy the comfort of coziness—being comfortable with your surroundings, with yourself, and with others. Let's look at each of these individually.

When you're comfortable in your surroundings, you feel safe and secure. When you're faced with being in a new environment, you'll often go through a period of adjustment

Chapter Two

where you're not 100 percent comfortable. This often happens when you start a new job, move to a new home, or visit a new place. If you're starting a new job, it is helpful to learn about the facility and the people who work there before your first day. It will help you to feel more comfortable if you can tour the building prior to your first day and meet some of the people you'll be working with in your job. Once you're at the new position, you will transition into feeling more comfortable with each day that goes by. Making an effort to talk to your new colleagues and connecting with them on a deeper level will aid in the transition. Being accessible and open will help coworkers get to know you better and, hopefully, they'll open up to you as well.

Are you comfortable with yourself? Being comfortable in your own skin means you're present and living in the now of your life; you're full of positivity and genuinely like yourself. Little things don't bother you and you feel a sense of peacefulness regardless of what you're doing. It's an overall feeling that everything is okay in your world. When you like yourself, you don't worry and are confident in your choices. Other people will feel drawn to you because you emit a strong sense of positivity. You're self-assured and go after your dreams instead of waiting for them to magically appear before you. Even though you're a go-getter, you never seem to be overly stressed out by situations that arise. You're an inspiration to yourself and to others. Being comfortable with yourself means you're cozy and content in your own spirituality; you know the path you want to walk and understand that there are lessons in every experience.

Coziness also means being comfortable with other people, as with gemütlichkeit (see chapter 1). If you're shy, there are some ways to feel more comfortable with others. First, look people in the eye when you talk to them. This builds a connection with them and makes you appear self-confident in your interactions, even if you're feeling uncomfortable on the inside. The more you practice this the less uncomfortable you'll feel. Just try not to stare someone down because then you might make them uncomfortable. Pay attention to other people's body language and how they're reacting to you, then you can determine your next actions accordingly.

Bringing a sense of coziness to your work, self, and other people will give you more positivity and happy moments in your life. Sometimes it may take a little work but it is well worth it.

TOGETHERNESS, WARMTH, LOVINGNESS, AND INCLUSION

If we make it a habit to be helpful instead of distancing ourselves from other people who are on the same path, it can add deeper meaning and a sense of coziness to our lives by creating joyful experiences for ourselves and others. We do not go through life alone. We all have friends and mentors, and we are interconnected to thousands of people during our lifetime. Some of these people are involved with you for your whole life, while others come and go. Experiencing the warmth of togetherness with the people you love, or even with those you encounter for a short period of time, not only shows others that you enjoy their presence but it also positively influences

Chapter Two

you on a soul level. When you are growing and moving forward on your own sacred pathway and sharing your divine light with those you meet, then you are involving them in your life and learning from them along the way.

Creating cozy situations with the people around you can be a lot of fun. If you're having friends over to your home for dinner try including everyone, giving them all a hand in planning the event or asking them to bring food for it, which allows them to be an integral part of the festivities. If you prefer to prepare everything yourself, then have meaningful and joyful conversations with your guests when they arrive. You can make deeper personal and cozy connections by including everyone in ways that allow more participation instead of just sending out an invitation to attend. The setting of your event can add more coziness to it as well. After dinner you could sit around in the living room having after dinner drinks, whether is coffee, tea, or something else, and simply enjoy one another's company and conversation.

When you meet someone out in the world that is a stranger to you, you can still experience a sense of warmth and togetherness by simply being nice to one another. A meaningful thank you when someone holds a door open for you may not seem like much but if your arms were full and it would have been a struggle to open the door on your own, then give a thank you that comes from your heart and a smile. You may even end up in a brief conversation. I remember so many times when I had to push a big double stroller through a door. People would hold the door open and we'd end up having a laugh over how big of a boat it was and how hard it was to navigate. Those were little moments of temporary togetherness, of sharing an experience with someone else that created good memories.

You have probably experienced the kindness of strangers many times in your life. In fact, showing random acts of kindness to others is something many people do in order to pay it forward. Paying for something for the person behind you in line is often done as an act of kindness, which may be returned to you in the future by someone else. Be willing to give of yourself by helping others in their time of need or anytime you want to do something nice for them. You don't have to have a reason to help someone and you don't have to know them. In their eyes, your kindness just might make them feel like you were an earth angel in their time of need.

There are some challenges that we need to figure out by ourselves in order to experience the growth they bring. Just remember that in the overall picture, none of us could succeed alone in the physical world without the assistance of others. Life can sometimes be a difficult journey, and that is why it is in our nature to be helpful to those around us. This helpfulness brings about a sense of loving togetherness. If we make it a habit to be helpful to others, instead of keeping to ourselves and distancing ourselves from other people who are on the same path, it can add deeper meaning, and a sense of coziness, to our lives by creating joyful experiences for ourselves and others.

LIGHT UP YOUR LIFE

There are many ways you can bring more light into your life to create an overall cozy feeling within your spiritual self and in your home or work environment. In your daily life, you can add

Chapter Two

more physical light by living in a home or working in an office with lots of windows. If you don't have windows, you can add lighting that brightens up your home or office. To get a cozy effect, you can use softer light bulbs, include a dimmer switch so you can increase or decrease the amount of light, and include beautiful light shades for a cozier effect. Add light and a feeling of coziness to any room by using candles or a fireplace that's wood burning, electric, or simply a video.

Have you ever bought a replacement light bulb and once you put it in the fixture it was way too bright or too dim? I have done this numerous times. The most important aspect of creating a cozy home is the lighting you use. If you're using 100-watt flood lamps in the ceiling you'll create an overly bright environment that seems clinical. Instead, choose lower wattages, and pick warm bulbs that bring out the red, yellow, and orange colors of the room, which makes it more comfortable and attuned to our historical connection to fire. Cooler light bulbs are brighter and often used in kitchens because they make the area look more energized and alert, and will make you feel that way too. Lighting can change the way your furniture and decorating appears to you. If you're not sure what kind of lighting you enjoy the best, buy a few bulbs in various wattages and lumens and try them out in your home. You may be surprised with the changes different light bulbs can make in how a space looks.

Physical light, from the sun or electricity, isn't the only way to add the sensation of light to a room. By using warm colors in your decorating, you can also enhance the effect of the lighting to add a cozy ambiance to the space. Including plants, sentimental items, pictures, pillows, throw blankets, and draperies to block too much natural sunlight increases the effect.

Now let's look within. Have you ever felt drawn to someone you don't know? Maybe you felt a connection to them because they seem to emit a lightness of being. They may be fun to be around, easy to talk to, or you just feel comfortable and at ease in their presence, as with gemütlichkeit (see chapter 1). What about people who are drawn to you? Do you find yourself having conversations with strangers in the store while waiting in line or with a telemarketer who cold-called you? We are all, at the core of our beings, made of energy, of divine light. When we are connected to our inner light and let it shine for all to see, we will attract others to us. The higher our frequency, the brighter our light shines. You'll often be attracted to others who are at the same or higher vibrational rate.

When you're aware of your inner light and are connected to your true spiritual nature, then you will grow spiritually and be more empowered to help others connect to their lightness of being on their unique path. When you embrace your own light, there is also a feeling of coziness, of being at home within yourself. When you learn to take negative emotions like anger, and feel it, acknowledge it, and let it go (on an internal level or externally process it in a constructive way such as starting a new project instead of taking it out on someone else), then you've made great strides in lighting up your inner essence, and in turn, your life on the physical plane. Connecting to your inner light is a way to begin any type of transformation that you want to make in your life. Remember: You are light, you are love, you are the true spiritual being that is you.

Chapter Two

CREATING A COZY HOME

Home is where your heart is. It's the place you live, where you go back to after a long day of work. It's where you're able to be your truest self. While we each have our own personal preferences about how we like to decorate our homes, a warm and cozy space that looks lived in feels much more inviting, comfortable, and calming than a stark space that looks cold and bleak. Creating a beautiful atmosphere in your home makes it something that you enjoy coming home to each day and that your family and friends will enjoy too.

Even if you prefer a minimalistic home, it can still appear warm and cozy even with only a few pieces of furniture. Keeping your design simple and then adding textured layers to your decorating often achieves coziness. You might have a thick throw blanket across the back of your couch, a leather-bound book on your coffee table, or a picture in a simple frame that brings the feel and theme of the room together. Items that are touchable, and often dissimilar, that draw the eye and hand, adds warmth as well. Bringing nature inside, using wood as an accent, strategically placing plants, and including seasonal natural items such as acorns, gourds, and fall leaves to create centerpieces all add coziness to your home. Simple lighting fixtures and just the right amount of decorations add coziness. Try not to overdo it, though. When you start adding too many items, you can make a room feel busy instead of cozy and harmonious, and then it can be overwhelming or feel cluttered.

Painting your walls in warm colors is another way to add coziness to your home. Stark white or beige walls are great for hospitals and offices but at home you want to add color to give the space character. Warm colors for the walls with splashes of bright colors used as an accent in your decorating, like adding an area rug, makes a room inviting, comfortable, and cozy. Maybe paint one wall a vibrant color to light up the space, or give it a Venetian plaster finish. Adding the appearance of texture to a wall with paint also adds coziness. Some of the ideas you might try are sponging with metallic paint, using a brushed pearl paint over the first color layer, color washing, wall mottling, rag rolling or sponge rolling, creating a linen weave, or adding a crackling effect. One of the coolest effects I've seen is when you use contractor plaster to create three-dimensional artwork on a wall. Creating a textured stone print on the surface of the wall is an interesting concept too.

Try It Now Exercise:
CREATING A COZY ROOM IN YOUR HOME

For this exercise we're going to create a cozy room in your home. You can choose any room that you like but for this exercise I'm going to give you some ideas to try out that will make your guest bathroom feel warm and cozy. Why the bathroom you ask? Because it can feel uncomfortable using the restroom in someone else's home. What better room to create a calm, cozy atmosphere for your guests?

Let's say that your bathroom is a full sized one instead of a half bath. In the space you have the bathtub/shower, toilet, sink with a cabinet with drawers underneath, and a linen closet. Some of you may have larger or smaller spaces but I'm just going with a medium space for this example. Now think of the look you want to achieve. Are you remodeling or just updating? Do you want the space to have clean lines, a specific

Chapter Two

theme like the ocean or forest, or something unique and different like the desert? Let's design one of each just for fun and to give you some ideas for your own design.

If you're remodeling and want to go with clean lines in a bathroom you'd want to use large tiles with minimal amounts of grout. Use acrylic glass on the outer shower walls to make the room look open and bigger than it is. Matching the color of your countertop to the tile, using similarly colored towels and a large shower head complete the look. If you're not remodeling, you could try painting the grout the same color as the tile in order to make it disappear at first glance. Use just a clear shower curtain that you push back against the wall when not in use and keep all of your stuff put away in the drawers and closet with the exception of towels and hand soap to keep the lines looking clean and fresh.

To create an ocean theme, choose a shade of blue that reflects the color of the ocean or of the sky. You could also start with a deeper ocean blue paint at the bottom of the walls and lighten it up as you move up the wall until you get a sky blue at the top. You could add stenciling of sea gulls flying at the top and images of sea creatures closer to the bottom. You might choose to use contrasting beige towels, mats or rugs that match the color of sand. For your shower curtain there are many sea-themed ones available with images of the beach, of fish swimming under the water, or whales rising out of the sea. Use sea-themed accessories to finish off the look.

If you'd like to create a forest theme, then add lots of plants to the bathroom. From hanging plants to potted plants, you can create an ambient forest atmosphere by adding greenery and ambient lighting. If you don't have room for real plants, pictures and a shower curtain with an image of the forest, foliage, or other scenery enhances the look and creates the same effect. Use wooden accessories, dark towels, and rugs to complete the experience.

For a desert theme, which I think is interesting because you're decorating a water area with the dryness of the desert, you could start with rich orange, red, and yellow coloring for your accessories, rugs, and mats. A shower curtain with red hued sand dunes depicted on it or a canyon scene would be a fun choice. Using accessories shaped like a cactus or made out of stone add an earthiness to the room.

Whatever theme you decide to go with as you remodel or redecorate your bathroom for your guests, remember to make it feel warm, comfortable, and relaxing to enhance the overall feeling of coziness.

COZINESS IN RELATIONSHIPS

Cozy relationships don't always have to be romantic in nature. When you experience coziness with other people, it is a warm sense of acceptance and camaraderie between you, even if you don't spend a lot of time together. There are many different types of relationships that we can have with other people. There are work relationships with your co-workers and boss, the relationships you have with teachers, professional business relationships, the relationships you have with service providers, with your neighbors, with delivery personnel and the list goes on and on.

There are numerous ways that you can ensure your relationships with people are successful, genuine, and filled with coziness. Start the relationship out with positivity based on trust. Have a mutual respect and appreciation for each other and avoid negative emotions. Understand that you'll never agree 100% on everything. Value and place importance on one another's opinions so you each feel that your thoughts matter to the other person. If you get mad, talk it out, explain the reasons why you're upset or angry to create an opportunity for discussion. Holding anger in can lead to negativity that festers and keeps coming back until one day, you either give up and walk away or explode.

If you're interacting with another person in a positive, genuine, and cozy way but you want to deepen those feelings even more, the key is in communication, respect, and being engaged with each other. Spending quality time together, even if that time is short, being open, honest, and asking questions if you need answers, allows you to have a stronger relationship with the other person.

Communicating with other people is more than simply talking to them. It's listening, understanding, and discussing your feelings about different situations. And it's the emotional discussion of feelings that really deepens the level of coziness between you and the other person. When you ask how someone feels about something—and you truly care about the answer—that's a deeper level of coziness than just skimming the surface with a generalized question. Sometimes discussing how you feel about a situation can be embarrassing or awkward but if you can work though those initial feelings to a deeper conversation, then it makes for a stronger foundation in your relationship, more fulfillment with each other and a longer lasting relationship.

Treating other people with respect is another way to build a good foundation. Being respectful means that you speak to each other with kindness, with genuine interest of what the other person has to say. Respect is being honorable to the other person, showing your appreciation for them. You show the other person that you respect their time, their feelings, their moral values and character, and trust them to show you the same courtesies.

Relationships can be fragile things. If you're involved in negative activities like calling the other person names, or talking bad about them to other people, then you don't need to be in the relationship in the first place and should probably end it. If it's a relationship that you can't end because it is work related or a teacher/student or similar situation, then it's important to find a way to make the best of the relationship within yourself so it works for you. Creating a cozy relationship can sometimes be very easy and then other times it can be very difficult, but in the end, you'll see and feel the difference in your interaction with the other person and feel glad that you made the extra effort.

CAN YOU BRING COZINESS TO WORK?

Creating a cozy environment at work can help you be more productive because you'll be calmer, focused, and experience less stress. Organization is one of the best ways to add coziness to your work environment, regardless of your career. If you know what you're supposed to do and when, you get the work completed in a timely manner, then your shift runs smoothly and without a lot of unexpected interruptions. That doesn't mean you're not going to have interruptions, but they can come

Chapter Two

with less stress or feeling of invasiveness. You can handle disruptions better because of your cozy frame of mind.

If you have an office or a desk, you can make changes to your space that creates an air of coziness in your work space. If you're constantly moving about in your job, then you can do things that make you feel cozy, like keeping a favorite item in your pocket that you can touch now and again to reconnect to your cozy feeling. I have this little stone that I found at a creek one day that I often carry around in my pocket. When I hold it in my hands for a few minutes, it makes me relax and remember the comfort I felt by the creek, relaxing and watching the water move down the stream.

Some of the ways you can make your desk or office cozier is to change the lighting to something more ambient and soothing by adding a lamp. I have lots of natural light in my office but I also have a lamp with a bulb that emits a softer, warmer light. If it's allowed at your job, you could also put a very small water fountain that will add a bit of white noise in your immediate work space. I also keep a soft fuzzy jacket nearby in the event that it gets cool in my office. It adds a feeling of coziness and I don't freeze. You might also consider adding a plant to your office. If a real one isn't allowed, a fake plant will still make the space feel cozier and you don't have to water it. Knickknacks and other personal items will make the area feel more cozy and homey. You might cover your work chair with a nice blanket or if you work in a cubical, decorate the walls with a cozy patterned fabric over the standard gray. Placing pictures of nature on the walls add to the overall feeling of coziness, too.

Another way to feel cozy at work is to make sure you're talking to your coworkers, developing relationships with them, and engaging in smiles and laughter whenever possible. If you're stuck at your desk all day, and sometimes that will happen if your workload is heavy, then it's difficult to feel cozy and easier to get stressed. Get up and walk around, chat with a colleague even if for only five minutes while on your way to take a break. It eliminates the monotony of the day. If your workplace allows you to offer suggestions to improve conditions on the job, then they're implementing the Japanese practice of kaizen (see chapter 1).

Doing your job with a sense of purpose, a desire to be successful, and giving 100 percent to your workday keeps you personally engaged in your job. If you go to work and just muddle through your day, then it's harder to feel happy with what you're doing and the sense of coziness you've created in your work space may not be enough to keep you feeling cozy inside. Take pride in your work, do the best job you can, and be of assistance to others if you can. You never know what someone else is really going through internally on a daily basis, and your help might be just the thing to make them feel warm and cozy inside.

COZY AMID THE CRAZY

Have you ever had a day that just went on and on and on with the craziest things happening that are totally out of the norm for your daily routine? Days like this can be a challenge to say the least. Add in people who are giving you a difficult time, who are being unreasonable, who just want to talk your ear off, or who are being needy and clingy, and your stress levels can shoot through the roof. How can you feel cozy in the midst of all of these things going on that are really out of your control?

Retreat. No, I don't mean running away from it all, but sometimes that sounds like a great idea, doesn't it? When I say retreat, I mean to take a minute to breathe deeply and go inside yourself, to connect to your spiritual essence and find the place where you feel calm, balanced, and cozy. Let yourself settle for just a minute and then continue on with your day. Sometimes when the craziness of the world is getting to you, the only place you can find coziness at a particular moment in time is when you connect to the coziness you carry around inside you everywhere you go. If a driver cuts you off or someone bangs into your shopping cart with their shopping cart or you feel bombarded by negative energy, then taking that breath and finding your center may be the only way to feel cozy in *that particular moment*. When you get home and have some time to yourself, then you can fix your favorite drink, soak in a warm tub, or do any number of things that feel cozy to you and release any negativity left over from the experience.

If you have to deal with high-stress situations, be strong, level-headed, and rational while it is happening and then later, to release the stress you've experienced, do something that is cozy to let go of those negative emotions. Maybe you could stop by the park on the way home just to take a walk or swing on the swing set. Maybe you could practice the Swedish concept of fika (see chapter 1) by stopping at a coffee shop or café just to grab a drink or have a bite to eat while you let go of the day's stress. Coffee shops have an air of coziness to them that will help you unwind.

In situations where someone is being unreasonable, unkind, or trying to pick a fight with you over something, try to remain calm. If you let your emotions run wild, then you'll really be in a stressful situation or an argument. You don't have to agree with the other person. Let them say what they want, listen to them, treat them as nicely as possible and see if there is anything that you can do to help resolve whatever situation they're experiencing. They may just be blowing off steam and need someone to listen to whatever happened to them that made them upset. Be the ear, then let it go once the interaction with them is over instead of allowing their negativity to affect you. Sometimes you'll be able to help them and sometimes not but you will have kept a level head.

Crazy days often make you feel crazy yourself, or you may feel overwhelmed, exhausted, and over it. These are the days when you need to take a little extra time for yourself at the end of the day to pamper yourself. Luckily, crazy days don't happen very often, and if you know how to connect to the feeling of coziness that you keep within you, it can help you get through the craziest of days.

THE ENERGY OF COZINESS

We all experience energy in different ways. Each person is unique, just as their own energy—their frequency—is distinctive to them. As you think of the energy of coziness, it is what makes you feel warm, safe, and happy inside your being. In countries where it is cold outside, the energy of coziness, of hygge, is a way to create a warm environment inside when the weather is harsh, cold, and unpredictable outside. It is finding affection, happiness, and contentment in the simple things of life and sharing those moments with family and friends.

To me, the energy of coziness flows in a spiraling motion, encompassing everything around it is a positive stream of slow-moving positivity. It feels warm and has a calmness about it that seeps into everything it touches. It sounds like the flow of water over rocks, sparkly and bright. It shimmers with light. When it touches you, the feeling of happiness brings a smile to your face. It can illuminate the darkness of a space and of your emotions. It makes you have realizations about yourself and about life that you may never have had if you weren't connecting with it. The energy of coziness enables you to find a peace within yourself that no one can take from you. It's ongoing and everlasting. It can settle in your soul and become a permanent part of your being that you can access at will.

Take a few minutes to think of a time when you felt cozy. What were your feelings? Were you happy and content to just be yourself without any expectations of how you should act or what you should do? The energy of coziness can eliminate the stress of expectations that others may have placed upon you. It allows you to rest, to relax, and to get to know yourself better. Coziness at the spiritual level helps you to understand your life purpose, to decide where you want to go in your life, and to find the path you will walk. It's lightness of being, slow-paced movement that can help you to slow down and truly enjoy your life.

The energy of coziness often offers a sense of renewal and of wellbeing that causes you to rethink your direction in life. When we take the time to slow down and really surround ourselves with the energy of coziness, letting it become part of us, its positive effects can brighten our mood and make us more appreciative of the little things in life that we may overlook. When connected to the energy of coziness, our outlooks can change. Things that we thought were problems no longer seem so bad.

To really connect to the energy of coziness, put yourself in a cozy room with ambient lighting, maybe some soft music playing in the background, some scented candles burning, and curl up in a comfortable piece of furniture like a chair or couch. Close your eyes and try to feel the cozy energy within the room. Once you connect with it, let it wash over you, move through you, and cleanse any negativity from you. Notice how it feels to you and call on it at any time that you need to feel a sense of renewal, coziness, and peacefulness.

GET COZY TO EXPAND YOUR CONSCIOUSNESS

Cozy living can help you to expand your consciousness, which is the process of connecting to your spiritual self, knowing you are a small part of a greater whole, and becoming aware of the many different aspects of your spiritual being while living in your physical body. It is the growth of the spirit to higher levels of awareness by understanding our own personal and spiritual truths. For each of us, reaching higher levels of consciousness means traveling different paths because we all have different lessons to learn. Cozy living can help you do this because of the peaceful, attuned nature of its energy.

Some of the ways that you can experience higher levels of consciousness through cozy living is to immerse yourself in coziness every single day. It is looking for the simple things, finding the beauty in the unexpected, and opening your eyes

Chapter Two

and your thoughts to ideas that you may have thought impossible before you started living a cozy lifestyle. It's not about the things you have or don't have but what you do to make your life feel more peaceful and connected to your true spiritual nature. Being true to your beliefs, intuition, and the things you enjoy in life is living a cozy lifestyle that expands your consciousness. If you do at least one thing each day that you like to do, that makes you feel cozy, then you're accomplishing your connection to a higher level of your own consciousness.

Being present, living in the moments of your life, and being more aware are catalysts to experiencing higher consciousness. They make you open your mind to the possibilities that there is more than what you're seeing, hearing, and feeling, and they urge you to explore what else is part of the whole that you haven't discovered for yourself yet. When you're present in your life it helps you to appreciate the people you know and the world you live in at a deeper level. You tend to look beyond just what you see to gain a greater understanding of what drives the people in your life, what makes them happy and how they interact with others. Being present allows you to also see these same things within yourself. Awareness and living in the moment helps you to release any fears that are holding you back from seeking higher levels of consciousness.

As you discover more, you're more willing to accept more, and in accepting more, you'll no longer settle for the mundane. Instead, you'll seek out ways to learn about your spirituality and try to understand all the universe has to offer. You'll begin to see the miracles of the universe in action all around you, which expands your consciousness even more. And all of this starts with feeling comfortable and cozy within yourself.

Expanding your consciousness takes time. It can take years, but if you start with creating a cozy environment, feeling coziness within your being, and expanding upon the energy of coziness that you've surrounded yourself with, then you'll continue to grow in spirit. The peaceful and warmth of cozy energy can cause dramatic increases in your consciousness. There is no limit to how much you can learn about your core essence, and who you are in spiritual energy, if you'll let the power you receive from cozy energy lead the way to expanded consciousness.

Try It Now Exercise:
CREATE A PERSONAL SANCTUARY

We all need a place that is our sanctuary. Many people today think of their home as their safe haven, but it's also nice to create a small space within your home that is uniquely yours—a personal sanctuary just for you. It is an area that is your space. It might be as simple as the corner of a room or even an entire room if you have an extra bedroom. It's a space that you can decorate in any way you prefer and the decor could be entirely different from the rest of the house. Your personal sanctuary is a place where you can retreat to when you're overwhelmed, or if the rest of your family is watching something on television and you'd just prefer to tune that out, and just read a book to relax. It is a place where you can enjoy some quiet, alone time and have a mys moment (see chapter 1).

Chapter Two

In your personal sanctuary, creating a clear uncluttered space will help keep the energy flowing in a positive manner. Bringing the outdoors in by adding potted plants will enhance the positive energy of the room. When you're in your private sanctuary, you can work on your spirituality—meditate, connect with your core essential self, or work on your intuitive abilities. Whatever you decide to do in your personal sanctuary, you want to make the decor appealing, cozy, calm, inviting, and completely your own style. You may enjoy soft background instrumental music to set a positive tone or you may just prefer silence. It will depend on your mood each day, which can change, so as you're setting up your personal sanctuary, think of the things you'll enjoy doing when in that space. You might have some books, a yoga mat, big fluffy pillows, or a giant beanbag chair. Incense or candles can add fragrance. Keep a variety of scents on hand to choose from to suit your mood. If you like to read, you could include a bookshelf for your favorite titles, runes, or oracle or tarot cards if you like to do readings for yourself. If the space has a window nearby, you could hang wind chimes and open the window on beautiful days. If you like to sew, do crafts, or do other similar activities, a personal sanctuary where you can work alone on your projects is a great way to keep everything in one space, stay creative, and have everything that you need at your fingertips.

Creating white noise in your personal sanctuary will help you relax. Consider a small indoor water fountain that you can place on a table. The sound of the water is soothing and can help aid in meditation or simply relaxing. You could imagine that you're sitting by a brook or a stream while listening to the movement of the water. Fans are another way to add white noise to a room or space, and they have the advantage of creating air flow. You can connect to the energy of the moving air while raising your frequency or, if you want to take a nap in your personal sanctuary, the air flowing over your body will help you sleep.

Remember that you're creating a personal sanctuary that is all yours, so anything that inspires you, motivates you, or makes you feel creative will help give the room your unique touch. Pictures and art enhance the feeling of coziness you're creating. Your personal sanctuary should help you release stress, relax, and enjoy spending time with yourself.

Chapter Three
MAKING COZY PERSONAL

Living a cozy life is a very personal situation for each of us and it will often be different from one person to another. What feels cozy to you may not feel cozy to someone else. To make it even more personal, take the time to go within yourself to learn more about your spiritual self and how coziness can help you reach both your personal and spiritual goals.

A CONVERSATION WITH YOUR HIGHER SELF

If I were to define the higher self, I would say that it is your core spiritual essence—the real you that is made of energy and light. It is the whole of your being, your complete consciousness; it is who you are when you're in the spiritual realm, the main part of your spiritual being that stays behind in the spiritual plane while another part of your being incarnates in the physical plane. On the earthly plane, we are but a piece of our whole selves. Just imagine how much knowledge you'd have if you discussed things with the main part of your energy that stayed behind in the spiritual realm to guide you on your journey here. Your higher self knows everything and can shed light on your path if you'll only ask for assistance. It knows the lessons you set out to learn in this lifetime because, as the whole you, you planned the life map you created prior to birth. Once born, the part of you that is experiencing the incarnation is always connected to your higher self (that's an unbreakable energy bond). It is the part you can seek guidance from at any time. Your higher self is the whole you, the complete you, the spiritual you, the light and energy you, the *real* you.

It's natural to talk to your higher self. Your mind does it instinctively all of the time when you're thinking about things and questioning yourself. If you don't know where to start, let's go over some things that will help you to consciously connect with and have a conversation with your higher self. First, you'll talk with your higher self in your mind's eye. You might imagine yourself sitting together somewhere in nature, in the Akashic Records, or anywhere that feels right for you to have a meeting with your higher self. The answers to the things you ask your higher self will feel as if they're coming from a place of wisdom, of higher knowledge, of infinite patience, and of understanding.

It's important to learn to distinguish between your higher self and your ego. If you're having a conversation with your higher self and the answers all seem to be fear based, petty, or have some sort of drama involved, then you're talking with your ego and not your higher self. A discussion with your higher self will never have any negative connotations. The information you receive will always be sage advice that will help you advance on your spiritual path.

Once you're able to connect with your higher self, do it often to keep yourself on the right course. Many times, our higher selves will reach out to give us messages, but we have to meet them halfway because they don't leave the spiritual realm. It's up to us to make the connection by raising our frequency so that we can get closer to where our higher self exists. Remember you can ask your higher self anything and get an honest answer because the higher self does not lie, fib, or color the truth in any way. You might not like what you hear in some instances but that's all part of the learning process and the purpose of being on the earthly plane.

YOU ARE SIGNIFICANT

Before you even picked up this book, you made the conscious decision to add more coziness to your life. So far, you've read about different ways you can make your life flow in a more positive direction simply by being aware of and implementing cozy factors into your daily existence.

It's important to realize the significance of yourself as you live a cozy lifestyle. No one else is exactly like you. Whatever steps you take to bring a sense of calmness, warmth, and positivity into your existence, it is yours and yours alone. No one else will do things the way you do them. If you haven't done so already, now is the time to embrace your own uniqueness by making a conscious decision to be your true spiritual self. Go after your own dreams, make plans that fit what you desire, and be loving and thoughtful to everyone else along the way. This is your life and you're in the leading role.

As you move forward, know that other people who live a cozy life are just like you. They don't have it all going for them, and they aren't luckier, more unique, or any different than you are. What they do have, and what you've been developing through understanding how a cozy life can be beneficial to you, is a keen sense of appreciation for all the bountiful gifts they are given in their lives. They've released feelings of frustration, anger, anxiety, jealousy, hatred, and other negative emotions. They see the blessings all around them and don't take anything or anyone for granted. It's all about your perception of the world around you and the people, places, and things in your life. It's about connecting to your soul essence on a daily basis and appreciating your own spiritual self.

For some people, embracing coziness is as simple as deciding to slow down and live a simpler life and then remembering to do something each day to connect to the coziness around them. For others, it is easier to write everything down and then review it in order to maintain forward motion. And there are those who plan out how they will add coziness every day for a week or month in advance so when they look at their agenda, they see a reminder to slow down and enjoy something cozy. It doesn't matter which method you use, whatever works for you is the best path to follow.

Embracing a cozy lifestyle also enables you to become more aware of things like playfulness, lightheartedness, spontaneity, affection, laughter, amusement, and cheerfulness. When you are aware of these special moments, you're able to cherish them even more. You'll feel conscious of every instance as it happens in the here and now, enjoying life to the fullest extent possible. It can change your entire perspective of the world you live in when you are aware of your spiritual self and are thankful for the gifts in your life. It will allow you to live your life to the fullest and filled with positivity. You are an amazing spiritual being. You are significant.

SELF-CARE OF MIND, BODY, AND SPIRIT

The world we live in is filled with both positivity and negativity. You see it online and on the television. Often the negative stories outweigh the positive ones. You also run into people during your daily life that can affect you positively or negatively, depending on their moods, the actions they take, or the words they say. These energies are all around us, so it's up to us to take care of ourselves in mind, body, and spirit. No one else will do it for you and only you know what feels appropriate for your own personal situations.

If you find yourself around negative people or in situations where you're uncomfortable due to the energy, you always have the option of leaving that situation. The darkness of negativity can't dim your positive light unless you let it. It can sneak up on you when you're not paying attention though. Once you realize what has happened, you can take steps to either change the situation or remove yourself from it. Changing negatives to positives can bring about transformational healing.

The self-care of your mind means realizing when you're overloaded, when you're not thinking clearly, or when stress is getting to you. Sometimes we can have so many things going on in our minds that it affects our ability to relax. You might be sitting quietly, but if your mind is going at one hundred miles an hour, then you're not really resting. When this happens, try to compartmentalize your thoughts and put them away for review at a later date. Worry is a big deterrent to a quiet mind.

Chapter Three

If you're worrying about something, try to decide if your thoughts are going to change anything. If not, think of a plan of action that you can do later and then put the worry away. This will help you find balance and ultimately rest your mind. If you try the Swedish practice of lagom (see chapter 1), which is moderation in everything, then it will help you find balance too.

Self-care of your body is just as important. If you're feeling sluggish or out of sorts, maybe you need to add some time to exercise in your day. If you don't have time to start a formal exercise program, maybe you could take a walk or park farther away when you go somewhere and get in a few extra steps that way. If there are things you've been thinking of doing to get healthier, go ahead and start them instead of putting them off. Maybe you need to lose or gain weight, stop smoking, or give yourself a makeover with a new haircut. The things you do to make your body healthier or to make yourself feel better about your looks are all ways to take care of your body.

Taking care of your spirit will enable you to find balance in your life. If you're lacking motivation, are unsure of your spiritual path, or just want to discover more about connecting with your spiritual self, then you can learn more by reading about the various elements of spirituality. Many times, learning about your intuitive nature, which we all have, or understanding about guides and the other side, may lead you to the path you're supposed to be traveling. I've always believed that we all experience a catalyst that steers us to enlightenment. It may be an illness, a near-death experience, or seeing something that can't be explained. When you take the time to seek your inner truth, take care of the body you've been given, and quiet your mind, you are caring for your whole being and moving forward in positivity. You may even experience a complete transformation both without and within.

WAYS TO APPRECIATE YOURSELF MORE

By definition, appreciation is recognizing and enjoying the good qualities of someone or something. While we often show our appreciation to others for their accomplishments, kindness, or helpfulness, we often forget to appreciate those same qualities within ourselves. It's easy to forget to appreciate ourselves, but it's important to remember that we need to do so every day. This isn't being selfish or arrogant, it's simply knowing that we're doing something good for ourselves, for someone else, or for the world.

If you look at someone who treats themselves well, who respects themselves, you'll notice that person is usually someone who respects others and treats them well too. This person puts value on their time, on their energy, and appreciates themselves. In order to live a cozy life and to grow spiritually, these are important qualities to have for yourself. If you expect to be treated exceptionally by others, then you should first treat yourself and others exceptionally. When you don't put value on your gifts, abilities, and your time, then you're not truly loving yourself at every level nor are you appreciative of your spiritual self. Loving and appreciating yourself is part of your path, embrace it.

If you're going through a difficult time, then you might say, "Melissa, how can I appreciate myself when everything is going wrong?" There are a couple of ways – first, when you

Chapter Three

appreciate the negative, you can transform it into a positive. If you're thankful for the lessons that you're learning through the negative incident, then it will help you see the experience in a different light. Secondly, negative situations, for exampling failing at something you're trying to do, can help build determination and stamina within you so that you continue until you achieve the goal. Winners and successful people don't give up. They keep trying until they get what they want. Negative experiences are never fun. You just have to choose if you're going to look at it positively or negatively—is a glass of water half full (positive) or half empty (negative)? I choose to always see it as half full. Embracing positivity, appreciating yourself and the situation you're going through, are ways to learn the most from the experience while working through it.

There are unlimited ways to appreciate yourself more but I'd like to give you some examples to get you started on your daily appreciation of yourself.

1. Appreciate your sense of humor because you bring happiness to others because of it.
2. Appreciate the fact that you're a good friend, compassionate and will lend a shoulder to cry on whenever someone else needs it.
3. Appreciate your honestly, your loyalty, your ability to listen and put someone else's needs before your own.
4. Appreciate the fact that you are filled with love and good intentions. You are accepting, giving, loving and always seek to make a difference in someone else's life or within the world. You work to create positivity in your life, to take the best care of yourself that you can,

and to be open minded while you're learning as much as you can.
5. Appreciate that you are who you are at a soul level by getting in touch with your higher self and your core essential self.
6. Appreciate that no lesson is to great or to small for you to learn on your life path.
7. And most of all remember that just as you appreciate other people, they appreciate you in return.

WORK/LIFE BALANCE

Part of living a cozy life is maintaining a balance between your job and your home life. Sometimes it's more difficult than you'd think if you have a particularly stressful job, if you have to bring work home often, and especially if you work from home or are an entrepreneur.

When you take time from your job to experience your life, then it refreshes you so that you are more productive at work. For example, as a writer it's important to live your life in order to gain information that you can share with others through your articles, blog posts, or books. If you're constantly writing, then you might run out of new experiences to write about. Writer's call this balance between work and home *refilling the well*. When you take time away from your work to refill your well, it enables you to feel more motivated when at work.

I believe that learning how to find a way to balance our work lives and personal ones is one of our big lessons during our lifetime. If you work too much, you might miss important events or spend less time with family and friends. After a while, you might start resenting your job simply because you feel it

Chapter Three

pulls you away from your personal life and family too much. This happened to me and I ended up completely changing careers because of it. If you find that you're no longer happy in your career because you can't achieve a good balance between your work and personal life, then if you can, a career move might be a good choice. If that's not an option, finding a way to balance the work load and your personal life is even more important for your well-being.

Finding balance between work and your home life can help you to work smarter in your job so that you can accomplish more while at work and have less need to bring it home with you. This leads to more productivity on the job and less to worry about when you leave the job. In turn this leads to more job satisfaction because you no longer feel it is cutting into your personal time.

Finding balance between work and your home life can help you to work smarter in your job so you can accomplish more while at work and have less need to bring it home with you. In turn, this leads to more job satisfaction and productivity because you no longer feel it is cutting into your personal time.

In order to live, we have to earn money to pay our bills so we all have to work. Being happy in your job, feeling committed to your employer, and feeling that you're a successful person who is doing a great job in your chosen field, is important to your overall sense of well-being. Having time away from your job to just be you and to have fun with family and friends is necessary because that's the core central you. We have to work to have money to live, but we have to live to be able to work. Finding ways to cope with the balance between the two can help you maintain a healthy relationship within yourself between the two.

Try It Now Exercise:
TAKE A ME DAY

Every now and then you have to make time for yourself. A wonderful way to accomplish this is to have a me day for yourself at least once a month. It's a day that you plan in advance if you've got a family, or if you're single that you can do on the spur of the moment. Tell everyone that you're taking a *me* day prior to the actual day. For this exercise, let's plan some things that you can do during your *me* day. You can choose to do anything you want to do. But, don't plan to go grocery shopping or to do any other chores. Instead, chose something enjoyable that you never seem to have time to do in the regular course of your day or things you want to do that no one else wants to do with you. This helps you to enjoy being with yourself, to pursue your own interests, and to have a stress-free, relaxing day.

So what kind of things can you do during a *me* day? You can sleep in or get up at sunrise, you can do nothing but lie around and watch movies all day long or you can go out and do things you've been putting off because they weren't necessary, even though you wanted to do them. Some people may enjoy a day at the spa; others might like to go to an amusement park, a museum, the beach, or any number of places. You might decide to work in your yard or just read a novel all day. Maybe you'll practice gezelligheid like the Dutch and spend the day getting out and about and doing some fun shopping or have fika, the Swedish coffee break (see chapter 1). Whatever you do, do it for yourself. There are times when you can have a *me* day with friends, which can also be called an *us* day. Maybe there's someone you are great friends with that will be in town for a day so you plan to spend the day together. It's always wonderful to get together with friends and do fun things.

If you don't have the time to take a *me* day, how about a *me* hour or a *me* morning, afternoon, or evening? Some *me* time is better than none at all. You might only be able to swing it once a month or every couple of weeks. Definitely try to make it more often than once every six months or a year. You need *me* time to decompress, to get back to yourself, and to think of the you that you may have lost along the way. Reconnecting to yourself is just as important as taking care of others or work or all of the other responsibilities we have in life.

We all need time to just be for our emotional and mental well-being. It is being able to enjoy our own company while doing things we like that allows us to truly feel our inner essence and to become reunited with our spiritual selves. You may not even realize that is what's happening but suddenly you're filled with a sense of contentment, of peace, and that all is right within your world, just because you're taking time for yourself and to reconnect with yourself.

CREATIVITY

Tapping into your creativity is a great way to add coziness to your life. Each one of us has our own unique creative talents and many different ways to be creative. It's up to each of us to let that creativity shine. For example, I'm an author and can write about many topics but I can't draw anything but a horse head and stick figures. Other people are wonderful artists but may not have any interest in writing. Some people are creative geniuses when it comes to marketing and advertising, while others use their creativity to make new discoveries in science. Whatever your creative talents, use them to enhance your life, which often will enhance the lives of others.

Being creative means making something out of nothing. It is turning an idea into reality. When I write a book, I start with a blank page. There's nothing there until I create words that flow together into sentences, then chapters, until I have a completed book. Painters start with a blank canvas. There's nothing there until they put paint colors onto the canvas and create an image. Take a minute and think about something you've done that is creative, where you've taken nothing but an idea and made it into reality.

Creative people share some similar characteristics, one of which is that they never, ever give up on their dreams. We are all creative, so that means we all have the ability to achieve our dreams. To know what we want and go for it. To move in forward motion and know setbacks are a lesson to learn from until we reach our goals. An artist might create many paintings to hone their craft, writers create many drafts before the final text is released. Creatives learn through trial and error, perfecting their creativity along the way. We are very curious and love to learn as much as we can about as many things as we can. We are usually very observant and notice things down to the tiniest details.

As you investigate your own creative nature, you will probably discover that you enjoy doing multiple things that are creative. A painter might also enjoy creating sculptures or participating in artistic dance. Inventors may enjoy taking

Chapter Three

things apart to see how they work and then put them back together again. A puzzle is fun for the creative person because putting all of those little pieces together creates a whole image.

To find your creative hot spot, think of the things you enjoy doing. If you like working with plants, then create a garden by planting seeds in the earth, tending those seeds as they grow into plants is a way to embrace your creativity. Or maybe you enjoy cooking. Inventing new recipes is a very creative activity. You might even become a world-renowned chef!

Anything that you can imagine and find a way to do is embracing your creative nature. If you're not sure what you're most creative at, then try lots of different activities to see what stimulates your mind, gets you thinking out of the box, and that you enjoy doing, and then follow through with the activity until you create something that is yours and yours alone. Every author has a different voice because they are unique individuals. Every artist creates unique designs with their own style and flair that reflects their inner light. As you embrace your creativity your work will shine with your own inner brilliance.

PRACTICE THE POSITIVE

It's easy to feel positive when things are going great; a little more difficult when things aren't going as well as you'd like them too. Times of transition and change can be challenging when you're trying to keep a positive attitude. You could fake feeling positive by plastering a smile on your face and having a cheery disposition, but if you're not feeling it inside, then you'll wear yourself out. What can you do to practice being positive so that you feel it deep inside instead of just pretending that everything is wonderful?

How about starting with a real smile? Smiles will make you feel more positive about things. When someone smiles at you, what do you do? Most of us will smile back. Smiles are contagious; they are a sign of happiness and joy. Taking the time to share a smile with someone else can lighten the day for both of you. A genuine smile is a little thing that can go a long way to feeling positive even if you're surrounded by negativity. Let the joy inside you escape in a smile.

Singing is another way you can practice feeling positive. Choose an upbeat song and sing to your heart's content. Singing is known to release endorphins that make you feel happier. It can lower your stress levels and just make you feel good all over. Have you ever been driving and your favorite song comes on the radio? What do you do? You sing along with it! Think about how you feel afterwards. Are you smiling? I bet you are! Singing helps you let go of worries and feel positivity.

Being aware of karma is another way to practice positivity. If you're treating people with respect, gratitude, and kindness, then you're interacting with them in a positive way. Inviting friends into your home to enjoy a meal, movie, or just spending time together is very cozy and is good karma. Being patient when you're waiting in line, or when a child is crying instead of being impatient, irritated and saying things that aren't nice will help you be more positive within your heart. Knowing how your actions and words affect others and taking a higher path is very positive in nature. That saying *what goes around comes around* is very true. What you put out into the Universe will

Chapter Three

come back to you so try to make sure that you're putting out the best you can so you will receive the same in return.

Think of a time when someone made a difference in your life. When they gave a helping hand, offered a shoulder to cry on, or did something completely unexpected that was helpful to you, when their support urged you on, helping you to become a better person. If you can pay it forward and make a difference in someone else's life, that's an awesome way to practice the positive. Even little things like holding open a door, helping clean up something that was dropped, or reaching something on a high shelf for a stranger in the supermarket can make little difference in someone's day while you're practicing positivity.

Being truthful, making amends with people, looking for that silver lining, and feeling the positive around and within you goes a long way to leading a cozy life. If helps you feel settled, balanced, warm, and in forward motion. Try to do at least one positive thing each day. After a while it becomes a habit and you'll be practicing the positive all of the time without even realizing it.

ROUTINES, RITUALS, NORMALCY, AND KNOWING WHAT TO EXPECT

Having a routine or ritual that you do every day creates a sense of normalcy in your life. You know what to expect and what's going to happen when, and you may seldom deviate from your routine. There's consistency, structure, organization, and reliability surrounding you when you follow a schedule. Routines are wonderful to have as long as you don't go overboard about sticking to them. If you're too stuck to your routine, people may refer to you as *set in your ways*. While there's nothing wrong with enjoying your routine, sometimes you'll have fuller, more enjoyable experiences if you shake it up a little by being flexible. To fine-tune your routine, look at what you already do and the times you do those things. If you notice a pattern in your day, then that's the framework of your routine. If you'd like to change it up some to add new activities, then take some time to rethink and restructure how you go about your day.

When you're creating a routine for yourself, it's essential to make time to do the things you love doing. This increases the feeling of coziness in your life. If you aren't incorporating the things you enjoy into your daily routine, then you might start to feel slighted, as if you're always doing for everyone else and never have time for the things you want to do. If that happens, then it's a good time to let go of the things you can to replace them with the things you enjoy.

Peacefulness in Solitude

Spending time alone is important for our spiritual growth and our personal well-being. Seeking the peacefulness in solitude is a necessary step in order to create a cozy lifestyle in today's world. This doesn't mean that you go into isolation for months at a time; it simply means that you take some time each day just for yourself to find and connect with the peacefulness within your own soul and in the world around you. Sitting alone or taking a long walk in the natural world so you can completely immerse yourself in your thoughts and the connection to your frequency and your spiritual essence is

Chapter Three

when the greatest ideas, revelations, and eye-opening concepts will come to you.

It's great spending time with family and friends, but you still have to have time to yourself to just be you and do something that you enjoy that connects with your spiritual essence. For example, an artist usually doesn't paint pictures with other people around unless they're doing a portrait. Writing is another endeavor that you do by yourself. Whatever you enjoy doing in solitude can lead to fantastic ideas from the universal stream of consciousness. If you decide to act on these ideas then they were meant for you, but if you don't take any action, then they'll go to someone else.

If time is a factor in getting some alone time, try getting up earlier in the morning. You can take your walk as dawn breaks, or you can sit in a quiet spot in your home and watch the sun rise. For me, early morning is a great time to write. I also tune into myself by using earplugs when there's a lot going on around me. This helps me to focus and find peacefulness in what can sometimes be a chaotic atmosphere. You could also plan dates with yourself—time when you can enjoy the solitude and peacefulness of being alone. You might think that spending time alone is the most boring thing you could do. I can understand this if you're used to always being on the go with a bunch of friends or family. When you spend time alone you're slowing down, connecting with yourself. It gives you time to just think about things in your life or things that you'd like to do, which in turn helps you get to know yourself better. Solitude gives you the ability to mull over problems and come up with solutions. Spending time alone is a great way to unwind and release stress, consider the life lessons you're learning, and connect with the creativity inside you.

It's Okay to Say No

Have you ever had someone ask you to do something, or hint for you to do something, that you really didn't want to do, yet you felt obligated to say yes to their request? When you're intuitive, especially if you're empathic, or if you're a care-giver type of person, then you might find yourself saying yes out of a sense of misplaced obligation or guilt. This is especially true if the person who's asking for the favor is a family member or a close friend. The majority of people like to be helpful and to make others happy. It's when you're unable to say no, which can be a problem for you, when you need to take action.

Let's first look at some of the reasons why we might have a hard time saying no to other people's requests of our time and energy. One of the primary reasons is because we feel we're not being the best person we can be if we don't do the things others ask of us. If our actions make someone else's life easier or helps them, that's great. But it is not our purpose to carry the burden for someone else or to give up our happiness to make their life easier and more carefree. This type of guilt—that we need to do things for others so they'll be happy regardless of how it affects us—is unhealthy and out of balance spiritually. We may also feel that if we don't do what the person is asking that we'll get into some kind of trouble, they'll no longer like us, or there will be some sort of conflict between us and the other person. This is one reason why some people take on too much work at their job. If you do a great job but never say no to extra work, then you could easily get overwhelmed. To stay in balance, we have to learn to say no to maintain your own well-being. Whatever your reason for avoiding the word no when people ask you to do something, it's important to realize when you need to start saying no if you're not feeling right about their request. Some people will try to manipulate you into saying yes, so make sure you're aware of this type of action; even if it's in hindsight after the request, you can learn from it and make a healthier decision for yourself in the future.

If you're continually saying yes then people may just start taking you for granted, which may lead to burnout and exhaustion. Let the people who are asking for help be responsible for themselves instead. Saying no to someone else's request might enable you to say yes when something is coming that is a benefit to you, or to you and another, not for you to always *do* for another.

Try It Now Exercise:
SOAK IN A TUB WITH CANDLES

Water is a necessary part of living. We need to drink it to stay hydrated, we need it to bathe and to cook, and it's popular for sports and other forms of relaxation. One of the best ways to regain your balance is through relaxing around water. Trips to the beach or a lake, taking a swim in a pool, or soaking in a Jacuzzi are fun ways to become one with the energy of water. There are times that you probably won't be able to get to the beach or lake and there's not a pool nearby, yet you may be yearning to experience that water connection. In cases like this, as long as you have a bathtub in your home, you can create a cozy water atmosphere.

You might think that you don't have enough time to take a long soak in the tub. If you can fit twenty to thirty minutes in your schedule, you can still reap the benefits of a cozy bath without having to use up a lot of your time. Then again, once you get in there you might just find yourself lingering. Taking a bath isn't just a female thing. Men can benefit from soaking in the tub too. Bathing is a great way for everyone to wind down and let go of the stress of the day.

When it comes time to take your bath, instead of just filling up the tub and sitting in it for a while staring at the walls be creative with the atmosphere. As the tub fills with water that is as hot as is comfortable for you, sprinkle in your favorite bubble bath, fragranced Epsom salts (which are especially good for helping sore muscles if you've been working out or doing manual labor), or baking soda and oils (to soothe your skin if it is dry or itchy). Scents can help you relax, and there are wide varieties of them for both women and men on the market. Check out the aromatherapy sections in your local stores for great selections. The heat of the water is also soothing to achy muscles and joints if you have arthritis, and the steam can help clear your nasal passages if you've got a cold. Light a few candles, take a glass of your favorite beverage to sip on, and turn off the bathroom lights. You'll create a cozy glow in the bathroom and around the tub, which makes your time in the water even more relaxing. Make sure you have a washcloth so you can soak it with hot water and then place it on your face. It's a great way to open up your pores.

Using intention during your bath can help you let go of negativity. As you're sitting in the tub, clear your mind of all the excessive chatter, stop thinking about the things you have

Chapter Three

to do, and instead just imagine your mind getting quieter and quieter. Replace your thoughts with feelings. Feel the water on your skin; its heat absorbing into your muscles. Watch the flickering of the candle flames, let their movements lull you into deeper relaxation. Now, once you're completely at one with the water and the cozy atmosphere you've created, feel the vibration of the water, allowing it to connect with your frequency and raise it.

As your frequency increases, it pushes all of the negativity that has accumulated within you out through your pores and into the water, where it is stabilized. At the end of your bath, you emerge from the water feeling warm, cozy, and invigorated while the negativity you left behind drains away with the bath water. Soaking in the tub surrounded by candles in a great way to relax and invigorate yourself after the stress of a long day or any time you want to regain balance within your spiritual self.

Chapter Four

EMBRACE THE MOMENTS OF YOUR LIFE

Every single moment during our time on Earth should be appreciated and not taken for granted. The people we spend moments with also deserve our thankfulness, love, and gratitude. When we embrace the moments of our lives, it gives us a new perspective on the things we may have taken for granted during the normal course of our day—things we might overlook simply because we're so busy. You might take the feel of the breeze through your hair, the sun on your face, or the song of a bird for granted because they happen all of the time. If you really notice them, your perspective will change and you'll become aware of them more and more often.

MEANINGFUL MOMENTS

When we think of the meaningful moments that we've experienced, we often think of the big moments, the life-changing events that affected us and caused a change in our path or in the status of our lives, such as graduating from school, moving out of our parents' home, getting married,

Chapter Four

having kids, the passing of someone you're close to, losing a job, getting a better job, winning awards or being recognized for your achievements in some way, and the list could go on and on. Some events motivate you to do more with your life, others cause you to pause and take notice of where you've been and where you're going, and still others make you more appreciative or realize you didn't know what you had until it was gone.

As you're considering the meaningful moments in your life, it's also important to look at the small things. Yes, big events can cause big change, but sometimes the little moments can cause profound change. Maybe you've experienced an unexpected surprise that made you trust someone a little bit more or a disappointment that made you rethink how you feel about expectations. Successes, victories, arguments, and losses all affect us in meaningful ways—even if you don't realize the meanings at the time. No matter how big or how small, when an event, person, or situation affects you in a meaningful way it's an opportunity to learn, to grow, and to connect with your core ideals.

To give you some ideas to jumpstart your search for the meaningful moments in your life, think about some of the following: things that others have done for you that were totally unexpected, places you've traveled to and the people you were with or met during the trip, successes that impacted your life, failures that taught you something, and the people you've known who made an impression on you or helped shape your life. As you review your past for the meaningful moments you may not have thought about in a while, also remember to purposefully create new meaningful moments in the future.

AWARENESS OF BEING IN THE NOW

An awareness of living in the moment, *the now*, of your life means to experience every single moment with a sense of heightened alertness. It is feeling the vibrancy of life, filling each day with positivity, and noticing what is happening around you. Being in the now brings about a sense of coziness because it gives you an appreciation of the people around you and the gifts from the natural and spiritual world. It is appreciating what you've been able to accomplish and obtain in life instead of focusing on what you haven't been able to achieve. Living in awareness and in the now means you're thinking about where you are right now in your life and what you're doing in this moment. You're not worrying about the past or planning for the future, but instead you're finding happiness and contentment with what you're experiencing today.

What does awareness mean to you? By definition, it is being perceptive and conscious and recognizing a situation, fact, or development. When applied to your life, it means to be more in tune with everything taking place. Consider your thoughts, emotions, feelings, actions, and how you react or don't react to all of it. Being aware enables you to see the truth of a situation, especially if you're linked to it through your intuition or a frequency connection. Being aware also means to be as informed as possible so that you can formulate your own thoughts about it. For example, if you want to raise your frequency, but you don't know what frequency is, then you will

Chapter Four

not be able to raise it because of a lack of awareness. If you learn about frequency and teach yourself to connect to the energy within you, your own personal vibration, then you can raise it because you're now aware of what it is and how it can positively affect you. The more you know in life, the more of a well-rounded person you will become and the easier it is to be more aware.

If you're not feeling a cozy connection to the world around you, then you may not be as fully invested in your own story, *your now*, as you could be. If you find yourself facing barriers to your forward progress, feeling tired and unconcerned with finding the positive, or being too focused on what you haven't done than what you've been able to accomplish, then it's time to make changes, to notice what is happening in your life, to become more aware of not only what is occurring around you but what is going on within you. When you are aware of yourself as a spiritual being that is made of energy, understand that you are timeless, and are more aware of what you're here to see, understand, and learn in this lifetime, then you will change your perspective. It's time to activate a connection to coziness, to *feel* life with all of your senses, which will help you live in the now. This will help you to see life in a different way; will encourage you to stop to notice the moments, like the rain streaming down a window pane, and to consider what you're experiencing and how it affects you emotionally and on a deeper, spiritual level. You'll feel a heightening of your senses during the experience. The more often you make yourself aware, the more aware you will become until it is second nature.

EMBRACING SILENCE

Making time for silence increases self and spiritual awareness. It gives you time to think about your intentions and to create plans of action to achieve your desires. When you spend time in silence, it heightens all of your senses. You begin to pay attention to your emotions, physical sensations, and what you see. If you're not talking and are sitting in a quiet room, you'll begin to notice other background sounds that you'd normally ignore, like the ticking of a clock, the hum of the refrigerator, or a bird singing outside of the window.

When I was in college, I got nodules on my vocal cords. The treatment was that I couldn't talk for a month. I thought I'd die! Miss I-Can-Talk-Your-Ears-Off wasn't going to be able to speak for a month? During the month, I went through about twenty notebooks because I had to write down everything that I wanted to say. It was difficult, to say the least, and when I was able to speak again I did it during one of my acting classes so that everyone could hear if there was a difference to my voice. My tone was clear, not hoarse and raspy like it was before I was diagnosed.

During that month, not only did I heal my voice but I also developed a great appreciation for silence. I noticed more of the things happening around me, more of the sounds that I didn't pay much attention to before. I also noticed how other people interacted with me when I couldn't talk. When you're forced into complete silence, you learn to appreciate the ability to talk and laugh. I learned a lot about connecting with my inner self during that time too.

Chapter Four

EMBRACING HONESTY

Honesty, in my opinion, is the most important character trait that any person can have. To live in coziness, we have to be honest with the people around us and, most importantly, we have to be honest with ourselves. It is a choice we make to not lie, use deception, cheat, or steal from another person. Honesty is a code to live your life by. Trust is built from honesty. When you're not honest with someone else, then you can hurt them emotionally, because, when they find out about your deception, they will no longer trust you. Being honest with yourself is just as important as being honest with other people. If you're miserable because of someone else's actions, if you're giving up your real self to be what someone wants you to be and you're not happy with who you're becoming, then admit that to yourself and take the steps needed to be true to yourself again. Denying how you're feeling, or the truth behind the actions of another person who isn't being honest with you, and thinking they will change to how you expect them to be, will only keep you in a state of dishonesty within yourself. See the truth of situations and people as they are, acknowledge them and decide honestly if the situation is right for you.

Moral values are one of the foundations for a cozy life. If you hold yourself up to high moral standards that are acceptable in society, the actions that separate right from wrong, then you will always stay on the side of what is right. If your moral standards are low and you go against what society believes is acceptable, then you'll often find yourself in trouble, not fitting in, or an outcast because you prefer doing bad things instead of good ones. Sometimes your values will be different than what is generally acceptable. As long as they are right for you and you're not hurting anyone or breaking any laws, then it is part of your path.

SIMPLIFY AND SLOW DOWN

Do you find that you're often moving at warp speed and still there doesn't seem to be enough time in the day to finish everything you want to do? Our society is very busy due to technological advancements that make it easier to connect to others around the world. This means your work day may no longer be one shift but could mean middle of the night meetings to accommodate a customer's time zone. For those of you with children, you may feel even more stressed due to their extracurricular activities in addition to your work. To find your way back to the simplicity of a cozy life, you should try to slow down and simplify.

When you're forced to slow down due to illness or some other life event, you start paying attention to the things you were missing when you were going full steam ahead. If you push and push yourself to the breaking point, then your immune system may become weak due to stress and cause illness or exhaustion. Instead of pushing so hard that you break, try to find balance. You'll be less stressed and ultimately more productive in the long run than if you're speeding along at a hundred miles an hour without any downtime.

To cuddle up to the cozy aspects of your spiritual being, start by doing an internal evaluation. Look at your past, your present, your talents, and beliefs. Do you really love yourself or are you pushing yourself too hard (which isn't really loving yourself) and missing moments you shouldn't have missed? Learning to love yourself and taking time to just *be* can be

Chapter Four

difficult especially if you've got a family to provide for and take care of. The thing is—you *have to take care of yourself* before you can take care of anyone else. So, put on the brakes, slow it down, and simplify your life.

You may be wondering what kind of changes you could make that will help to simplify your life. Let's go over some examples to get you started. Look at your time commitments and how much you're multitasking just to get it all done. There are only twenty-four hours in a day and if you're busy for seventeen of them and get seven hours of sleep, then there's no time to relax. What can you let go of completely or do less frequently? Find as many ways to free up your time as you can so that there is some time for you. For example, instead of waking up and looking at social media on your phone, you meditate, begin the day reading a few pages from a book you enjoy, or do some stretching exercises.

Take a look at your stuff. Is your home cluttered with things that have accumulated? Start donating items you don't need and organizing the ones you do need. The cleaner and more open your living area is, the more cozy and relaxed you'll feel. And finally, let go of the technology for a while. When you disconnect from being constantly available to everyone then you'll have more of a chance to breathe, smell the coffee or roses (whichever you prefer), and settle into a cozy feeling within yourself.

Try It Now Exercise:
SIT QUIETLY AND WATCH

Hygge includes being aware of the moments in your life, which is one of the best ways to begin the path of transformation. You have the ability to make a total transformation within yourself if that's what you truly desire. It is getting back to the truth of your soul and being mindfully aware of the world around you. In this exercise, I'd like for you to select a place where you can watch nature and contemplate what you're seeing and feeling.

When you take the time to sit outside in a natural environment, it's easy to quiet your mind and consider the moments of your life. This is living friluftsliv (see chapter 1). Think about the different moments you experienced during the day. Try to go through a few different emotions to see if they occurred that day. Did you have a moment that made you happy? Maybe you saw a puppy or a funny video that made you laugh. Maybe you experienced a situation that made you feel a little melancholy or sad. Did you have an argument or lose your temper? Think of each of these different emotions and the situations that occurred. Can you dig deeper to see why you reacted the way you did to those situations? If you can, then you're experiencing growth at a spiritual level.

While you're sitting in nature also pay attention to the now of that particular moment. Feel the moment, the energy of the world that surrounds you, and the way it makes you feel inside. First focus from the greatness of the sky, trees, ocean, or whatever environment you're in and connect your spiritual self to the spiritual essence of your surroundings. Just feel. Now take your focus smaller to notice more and keep taking it smaller until you notice the little things around you. Do you see

Chapter Four

small rocks? Is there water, any interesting plants, or maybe bugs crawling around? As you experience the now of your moments in nature, allow its energy to balance you and refresh your mind, body, and spirit. Your observations may surprise and enlighten you.

For the next phase of this exercise find a place where you can observe a crowd. You might visit a park, mall, or anywhere that you'll encounter people. You can learn a lot about human nature this way. You may recognize yourself in the actions of others. You may find yourself empathizing with someone who seems lonely, sad, or upset if they remind you of a day when you weren't at your best emotionally but had things you had to do. A kind word to them as you pass by might just make their day. I tend to do a lot of observing when I have to wait in line. To me it's interesting to notice how those around me are interacting with one another or with me. I can't tell you how many conversations I've struck up with people while waiting in line. You just might learn something new from those interactions that might help you in your own relationships. Watching people with animals can be enlightening too. I've always believed that how a person treats an animal will tell you their true nature. The next time you have to wait, observe those around you to learn more about the way we all live together on the planet. Your observations may surprise, entertain, and enlighten you.

LEAVE TECHNOLOGY BEHIND

Technology is wonderful, isn't it? With the technological advances of our society it's easier than ever to get our work done quickly using our desktop computers, smartphones, laptops, and tablets. There are apps for just about everything, from creating a grocery list to maps to find our way around this great big world we live in. There are apps for every age group, for every professional field, for entertainment, and for sports. It enhances our lives, making many of the tasks we do daily easier and quicker to accomplish than ever before.

We no longer have to visit the library to do research; we can do it online through a wide variety of search engines, websites, dictionaries, and encyclopedias. Yet, sometimes, it's refreshing to visit a library and read through a wide selection of books to learn from the authors who took the time to research and write about every topic imaginable. You can even find rare and out of print books at online retailers. The feel of holding a book in your hands and flipping through the pages gives a sense of comfort you don't get when using handheld devices, a laptop, or a desktop computer. You can now attend school online, which makes it easier for people who have to work full-time to earn a degree.

Technology has wonderful advantages, but just like everything in life, there's a flip side to it where disadvantages come into play. One of the primary things that you'll encounter is that some things you see online aren't true. You might think it's true but upon further research, you discover that it's not. I remember once when I believed a story about a miniature giraffe. Looking back, it's funny, but at the time I was amazed that miniature giraffes were in existence. Image editing software has come a long way over the years and that little giraffe looked so real! Yes, I was gullible, I believed it, but it taught me an important lesson. Now I think twice before falling hook, line, and sinker. Now I fact-check stories if I'm not sure that they're truthful. It's easy to let technology do the work for us that we used to do ourselves.

When was the last time you bought and used a paper map? For me, it's been years because it's easier to use GPS (global positioning system) to map out where you need to go. The disadvantage of this is that you can end up in the wrong place if you're using outdated software.

Another disadvantage that I find with technology is that people are having less face-to-face interaction. You can see two people sitting side by side, both on their cell phones, only to find out that they're texting each other. Instead of doing that, why not put the cell phones away and have an actual conversation with one another? People often sleep with their cell phones beside their bed or they have their laptops, tablets, and phones in the bed with them. Why not turn those off, put them in another room, and get a good night's sleep? Some people even get addicted to technology and have withdrawal symptoms if they have to be without their smartphone for any length of time.

Technology is a wonderful addition to our lives. Try to use it to enhance your life without getting addicted to it, ignoring other people because of it, or letting it take over your day.

SOCIAL MEDIA

Social media is one of the great advantages of the Internet and one of the technological advances made in the things you can do online. Through social media we can stay in touch with family and friends, even those we have lost contact with over the years, and meet new people all around the world who have similar interests. Today most people are active on one or more of the social media platforms. Social media can give us a sense of coziness through connections with others. We can also obtain news stories through social media and keep up with what is happening in the world. Sharing pictures has never been easier, so you can see events you couldn't attend in person.

It's up to us as to how much time we spend online. It's important to know that while social media has tremendous advantages, it can also become a huge distraction. Have you ever found yourself on a social media platform just scrolling down your feed looking at funny videos, memes, or seeing what your friends were up to last night when you really are supposed to be doing work? I know I have. Social media can become a waste of time that we could use being more productive. It also makes us lose focus. When you get so wrapped up in social media that you pay more attention to it than you do to what's happening in your real life, that's when social media becomes a problem. Social media can expand your horizons. I have online friends all around the world who I have never met face-to-face but who I consider my friends. Some I have been connected with for years. Some I met through our businesses and I've stayed in touch with them through social media. It's a great way to stay connected and to learn more about your world and the people in it, as long as you make sure it's not the only way you engage with people. Doing things with your family and friends without your phone attached to you will help you find balance in your online life and your real life.

Chapter Four

Try It Now Exercise:
GO TECH-FREE FOR A WEEK

Oh no! You did *not* just say to go tech-free for a week, did you? I must have read that header wrong. I can't live without my phone! Please say you're kidding me...

What was your first thought when you read the title of this section? Now be honest. Did you react like the first paragraph above or did you think *no big deal*? For me, giving up technology isn't a big deal because I don't depend on it for my livelihood or entertainment. Half of the time I forget to take my phone with me, which frustrates other people, but hey, that's just me. I'm not attached to the thing. If you use your cell phone for work, which is the case with many people that I know, then you'd have to schedule your tech-free week during your vacation. You can talk to everyone who is important in your life and let them know what you're doing beforehand; change your voicemail message to say you're on vacation and tech-free this week and you'll get back to them when you return.

So you've got the cell phone covered. Computers, including any handheld devices like e-readers, are off limits too. Shut them down and put them away. Avoid any opportunities to get online on a public computer. Tech-free means you're off the phone, computer, video games, social media, and any other technology. You're unplugged from the distractions of the Internet and social media, which can eat up a lot of your time doing nothing. You're going grassroots, back to the basics, back to a simple life, back to cozy, and back to you.

For many people, technology is all they know. They've grown up surrounded by technology. This exercise is going to more difficult if this describes you. You may think you can't live without your phone, but I assure you that you can, even celebrities practice weeks without technology and rave at the results they achieved. Sure, your online friends will miss you while you're gone, but just remember that saying *absence makes the heart grow fonder*. Now comes the fun part—getting to know yourself better and truly experiencing the people in your life and your surroundings.

So what do you do during your week without technology? The first thing you'll do is adjust to not reaching for your cell phone. You'll probably experience boredom and possibly feel short tempered the first day or two. Once you get used to not using technology, you'll begin to find other ways to entertain yourself and to get information, and you will probably feel more relaxed as you take in the real world around you. You'll find you're able to maintain better focus, you're more attentive to your surroundings, and you're more productive in your tasks when technology is out of the window. Unplugging from technology can help you get your priorities in the right order, enjoy more time with family, and enjoy activities that allow you to meet new people in person, rather than online.

If you don't think you can let go of technology for a week then just try it for a day. There are so many benefits to unplugging, even if it's for a short time. You might even prefer having less time online and more time doing things in your everyday life.

LIVING IN THE MOMENT

When you live in the moments of your life you look at everyone, everything, and every situation with fresh eyes. You look for details that you normally wouldn't see. If you're

Chapter Four

keeping a journal, write down what you notice in these moments. You may pay more attention to the beauty of a sunrise or sunset or the smell of flowers in the air. Songs may have more significance when you really listen to the words.

Living in the moment is easy to do once you get the hang of it. Take a look at your surroundings. Is there anything or anyone near you that you've taken for granted lately? We usually don't think about having a roof over our heads or how warm and cozy our beds are when we finally get to lie down to sleep. What about that hot water in the shower? Living in the moment means to be aware and thankful of the gifts you've been given. Think about your mother's perfume or father's cologne. If you catch a whiff of that scent when you're out shopping does it immediately remind you of your parent? Being able to notice that scent and to stop to think about your parent for a single moment in time—that's living in the moment. If you didn't have a great relationship with your parent, then acknowledge the scent, think about the accomplishments you're proud of and how much you've been able to do in your life, and then let it go. That is acknowledging the moment for what it is and then releasing it out into the universe so it doesn't have a negative effect on you.

Reconnecting to your spiritual essence is a way to live in the moment. Because you connect to the divine part of your inner self, you are surrounded with your own positivity and light and the frequency (the vibration) that is uniquely you. This makes living in the moment easier and more meaningful.

Taking deliberate and specific actions will help you stay focused on the moments of your life. Let's say you're in the middle of your work day. You're writing up a report but you're so tired your eyes keep closing. Instead of fighting it, give into that moment. Let your eyes close and just listen. Do you hear yourself breathing? What other sounds are happening around you? Can you hear the air conditioning or the murmured speech of coworkers? Maybe there's a clock ticking or someone is tapping on their computer keyboard. Listen to all of the things happening around you that you normally wouldn't be paying attention to. Now let your mind move into your own frequency and into your inner essence. Let the cozy feeling of being at home within yourself rejuvenate you and refresh your senses. You feel energized, aware, and in tune with your inner self. There is a sense of balance because you connected to the moments happening around you. Open your eyes. Now you're ready to finish that report and will be refreshed and awake while you do it.

EXAMINE THE LITTLE THINGS

Life is filled with big, eventful moments that make memories that last a lifetime. It is also filled with little moments that can be easily forgotten. Sometimes those little moments can be the catalyst for big changes in your life. Realizations are often spurred by some little action, resulting in moments of clarity.

Spirituality has, at its core, a foundation of warmth and love that is part of our overall well-being. When we are more spiritually conscious, we're able to change ourselves and improve on all levels, including the spiritual, physical, and emotional. Our self-esteem soars and feelings of self-worth increases. With it comes a calm peace of mind that can help us be a positive influence on others. When we experience this type of calming, cozy effect because we are connected to our

Chapter Four

spiritual self, we can consciously deepen our spiritual foundations, can have better relationships with others, and do not take things or people for granted. Looking for the messages in the little things can help us grow as spiritual beings regardless of other things that are happening at the same time. Being mindful of these small moments makes them extra special and more meaningful.

How do you start your examination of the little things, those unexpected moments that often lead to eye-opening experiences? Begin by noticing more. As an example, let's say you're at a store. If you're shopping in a hurry, you go in, grab what you need, and leave quickly so you can get to the next thing you have to do. It's efficient but you miss a lot of what is happening around you when you're fast-tracking it through the store. The next time you go shopping, allow yourself extra time just to stroll down the aisles and look at things, notice the people around you, and see if you discover anything interesting and new. I know when I do this I often end up in conversations with strangers about something on the shelves.

Recently, I was looking for a disposable cake holder that I could leave at an family event. Near the plastic containers was a display of cups with straws in them. Every lid was movie character themed. A few minutes later a mom and her child stopped to look at the cups. The child picked up two and wanted them both but the mom said she's only buy one. The child looked at me so I smiled at her and then she asked me which one I liked better. That ended up in a conversation between all of us about the various movies—had I seen this one and that one and which was my favorite character—but if I'd chosen to ignore that little moment of that child looking at me, and if I'd chosen not to smile at her, the conversation would have never happened. In the end, she chose a pretty blue cup with snowflakes. By acknowledging a little moment, I had a wonderful experience with a mom and her child.

You too can have similar experiences by noticing the people near you, offering a smile, or saying hello. Or by feeling the wind in your face or the rain on your arms, listening to the song of birds, hugging a puppy or cuddling a kitten, watching the sun rise or set, or just going for a drive to experience the environment. There are little moments all around you if you'll be aware and notice them. Little moments can open your mind and heart to many wonderful things.

MINIMALISTIC APPROACH

The minimalistic approach to coziness can help you enjoy more of the moments of your life. But what is the minimalistic approach? It means to enjoy more by having less, similar to the Swedish concept of lagom (see chapter 1). It is appreciating the things you have and not constantly striving to get more stuff. Is it using what you need instead of having a lot of things that are unnecessary. It's spending less, doing less, needing less. If you're unsure if you'd like to live according to the minimalist approach, you can try it for a short time to see if it works for you before taking it to the extreme and giving away all of your belongings and moving into a tiny home. Living minimally means different things to different people, so you have to determine just how minimal you want to go in your downsizing.

To try being a minimalist short-term, you can first start by getting rid of all of the clutter in your home. Clutter blocks the

Chapter Four

flow of energy in a space and removing it allows the energy to flow freely again. Once the clutter is gone, you can also sort through your clothes and donate items you no longer want or that no longer fit you. Do the same in your kitchen. If you have accumulated ten spatulas, then leave one out and pack up the rest. Go through your home doing this in every room. Put things in boxes and pack them away in a spare room or garage until you decide if you really want to pursue living the minimalistic lifestyle. Once everything is put away then your home will be simplified with less clutter, less decorations, and less duplication.

Now think about the other things you can do without that will also save you money. If you go to the movies or out to eat a lot, decide to cook at home and forfeit the entertainment for a while. Are there other luxuries you can eliminate? If you stop at a coffee shop every morning, try making your coffee at home. When you go shopping, make a list first so you only buy what you need instead of a lot of extras. Choose items that are versatile instead of buying many different items that serve the same purpose.

Once you've cut back on your spending and reduced the clutter in your home, then start thinking about how you can be a minimalist in the rest of your life. If you're doing too much, choose to eliminate some activities. By eliminating stressful situations, activities, or people who cause you anxiety, you'll more easily be able to stay balanced. Maintaining a peaceful, calm attitude is crucial for a cozy lifestyle.

Living with a minimalistic approach to life isn't just about the things you have and the things you do. It's about cutting back to what you need, eliminating things that make you worried or anxious, and surrounding yourself with people who fill your life with happiness. You may find you really enjoy the minimalist approach, but if you don't, then just pull out those boxes and put your stuff back in its place. You'll never know how you feel about it until you try.

CLUTTER CAN HOLD YOU BACK

A cozy environment is not a cluttered environment. Clutter can accumulate without you even realizing it is happening. Mail piles up on the table, junk drawers are suddenly filled to overflowing, and stuff is just sitting around. Clutter can be a great catalyst to get you into a cleaning spree, but it can also hold you back from experiencing the free flow of energy throughout your home or work space. It's hard to feel cozy when clutter is taking over. Organization will prevent clutter from holding you back from the coziness you desire in your life. When your stuff is organized, it is neater and there is less of a mess in your environment.

Emotions can also cause you to create clutter. Maybe you're holding on to clothes that are too small because you want to lose weight. In a situation like this, consider how old those clothes are. If you've had them for seven years, and they're a size 1 but you've been a size 10 for all of that time, then maybe it's time to donate them and feel happy with your size 10 body. Items like mementos, pictures, and birthday cards from people who are special to you might be things you'll want to keep. Cleaning out the clutter in your environment helps you feel calmer and more relaxed.

Now it's time to address the clutter in your mind. When you have lots of thoughts happening at once, it can get

Chapter Four

overwhelming. Grab something to write with and a piece of paper. The easiest and fastest way to clear your mind is to give those thoughts importance on paper. Write down that to-do list going through your mind. Once it's on paper, you'll find that you're no longer going over it mentally because you have it right there in front of you. If you think of something else, add it to the list. That way you can think about the things you need to think about instead of constantly sorting through a ton of different thoughts.

Letting go of clutter is just like letting go of the things that no longer serve you. It brings balance so you can move forward. You only have so much space in your life for emotions, people, etc. In order for new opportunities to come into your life, you have to let go of the things that aren't serving you. When you release it, energy flows with positivity, your mind calms and gets quiet, and you can move forward on your spiritual path with purpose.

Releasing What No Longer Serves You

Just as clutter can sneak up on you and affect the positive flow of energy in your life, emotions, and perspective, people can do the same thing. There comes a time when you should evaluate all areas of your life to see what has accumulated that isn't serving your best interest. A full cup will overflow when it can't hold anything else. When you're holding on to things that no longer serve you, the same thing happens to you. There's no room in your life for the new if the old is taking up all of the space. Living cozy means to live simply, to let go of negativity and the things no longer serving you in order to find peace, happiness, and joy in all areas of your life.

I make it a practice, especially when I'm feeling overwhelmed, to look at what I'm doing that isn't working—that is no longer serving me. We can release anything we no longer need, even if it is difficult. It is all based on your desires, needs, and priorities, which often change over time. Letting go of what no longer serves you doesn't mean to let go of everything. If something has already served its purpose and is now just taking up space in your life, then it probably needs to go. I tend to work too much. I always take on a lot of different projects at one time and sometimes I end up doing so much that I find it difficult to relax, slow down, and just enjoy some cozy time. When this happens, I know it's time to let things go so I can slow down. I've had to learn to delegate responsibilities. This was difficult for me because I want to be there for the people in my life. Delegating not only helped me have less to do but it helps others learn to be more responsible.

If you're not sure how to let go of the things that no longer serve you, think about this—does it make you happy, do you feel like you're accomplishing something and making forward progress, does it serve a purpose, and what would happen if you let it go? I love lists, so I often write all of these things down, evaluate it, and then make my decision. This evaluation should also include people. If you have people in your life that you know don't have your best interests in mind and are only around you because they want things from you, or if they're always negative without anything positive to say, or maybe they're drawn to drama. If any of these are true of someone you know then consider what your life would be like if they weren't part of it. Would you feel relieved because you don't have to deal with their drama, their negativity, or their using

Chapter Four

you anymore? If allowing someone a place in your life is no longer a mutual, equal relationship, then maybe it's time to move on. On the other hand, if someone no longer wants to be part of your life, let them go.

Emotions are another area where you have to let go of what's no longer serving you. It's practically impossible to live a warm, cozy, simple life if you're harboring feelings of resentment, anger, or jealousy. The two don't mesh very well. Negative emotions affect you on a soul level, lower your frequency, and can keep you feeling out of sorts. When you release that which no longer serves you, then you're opening the door for new, exciting, and positive things and people to enter your life.

TODAY IS TOMORROW'S YESTERDAY

So let's think about that heading for a moment. *Today is tomorrow's yesterday.* We can also rephrase it to say tomorrow's yesterday is today. By tomorrow today is yesterday. Or how about today is yesterday's tomorrow? As you contemplate the play on these words, think about what they mean to you. To me, it means to appreciate the time we have today, don't put off until tomorrow what you can do today, and that time moves forward and days slip into the past regardless of what's going on in our lives, what we have to do, or how much time we think we have to do them.

Time is relative. If you really think about it, it is an illusion that was created to help us mark the seasons, to define the space between one sunrise until the next into sections that help us organize our days into hours minutes and seconds. So, if time is relative, wouldn't yesterday, today, and tomorrow be relative as well? It's all in how we look at it. Each of us has a unique perspective when it comes to time and the passing of time. That's why it is so important to live in the now of your life, to appreciate the moments you are given as you experience them. Act in the moment, do things you should do, offer an apology, give a hug, and tell someone you love them. That moment in time will never happen again. Don't lose an opportunity to say the things you want to say to people because you might not get the chance at a later date.

Things in the past have already happened and are out of our control. What's done is done and there's nothing you can do to change it. Worrying, wishing you'd done or said something differently, isn't going to make it anything other than what it is. When you hold onto worry or regret, you're holding onto negativity which can make your frequency lower and make it harder to live in the spirituality of coziness. Acceptance, determination to make something better out of the lesson you learned, and the ability to forgive yourself for your mistakes or perceived mistakes, is a way to increase your frequency and to move forward on your spiritual path.

Forgiving those who have hurt you will also enable you to move forward in positivity while embracing the coziness within your spiritual self. That doesn't mean you have to continue to be around the person. Sometimes the best way to leave the past in the past is to make a clean break and let it all go. Yeah, I know that's easier said than done. Remember that you can't change anyone, it must come from within them, and people always show their true colors eventually. You deserve all that you can achieve in life and if other people don't have your best interest at heart, it might be time to just let them go.

Chapter Four

Each day you have the chance to be the best you possible. You can hold your head up high and know that you're giving yourself every opportunity to excel in whatever you want to make of your life. Make the most of your moments. Don't let time slip by you and then suddenly you wake up one day full of regrets for the things you wish you'd done or that you wish you hadn't done. Instead of wasting the time you've been given on Earth, make a promise to your spiritual self that you will learn as much as you can, you'll do as much as you can, you'll be the best person you can in every possible way, and you will not let anyone hold you back so you'll progress on your spiritual journey.

IMPULSIVE BEHAVIOR

Impulsive behavior is when you speak without thinking it through or take action based on how you feel instead of rational logical thinking. It is normal human behavior that makes life fun and interesting. We all decide to do things on the spur of the moment, it's part of being in the now of your life. We all have gut feelings and intuition that guides us and that can drive our impulsiveness.

I've always been an impulsive person. I'd get an idea in my head and off I'd go. I couldn't begin to tell you how many times I drove from Florida to Virginia just because I decided I wanted to go. I'd just pack my bags, get in my car, and drive. Being impulsive adds a sense of adventure to your life. It gives you the feeling of freedom, of being true to yourself and of going after what you want in life. Most of us know when to control our impulsive nature. For instance, I wouldn't take off on a road trip right now because I have responsibilities at home that I can't shirk off. But if I didn't, and the urge hit, well, that's different.

When we allow our impulsive urges to overtake our responsibilities, that's when it can become a problem. It's important to know the difference in being impulsive and recognizing impulsiveness that's gotten out of control. For example, someone who likes gambling might allot a certain amount of money from their pay each week for gambling. For the impulsive person who has gotten out of control, they might just spend their whole check. Being impulsive isn't bad as long as you don't let it control you. If you keep your impulsive nature in check and don't go overboard with it, then you'll discover that being impulsive makes you happy because you're in touch with yourself at an emotional level and you trust in your feelings. You know what you want, what you need, and how you're going to get it. Being impulsive adds fun to everything and impulsive people love having a good time. An impulsive person doesn't hesitate to be adventurous. You don't have to twist their arm because they follow their hearts, wants, and desires. Since they often move from one thing to another quickly, impulsive people don't procrastinate much. Sure, they make mistakes due to their impulsiveness, but boy do they have fantastic stories to tell about their adventures.

Some people prefer to squash their impulsive natures completely. As with anything, there has to be balance between never being impulsive and always acting on impulse. This is one area where it's okay to be in the middle instead of being too much on one side or the other. In other words, moderation is better than going to the extreme. Sometimes fear can hold us back from acting on our impulses. If you're worried about what

Chapter Four

other people might think or say about you, then you may find yourself being less impulsive. Also, fear of taking action can hold you back if you're afraid of what the results of those actions will be. People who consider the results of impulsive behavior before taking action have achieved balance in their impulsiveness.

THE FREQUENCY OF A MOMENT

Throughout the universe, energy is in constant motion every single moment. Energy is required in everything we do, every thought we have, and every physical movement we make. This energy is the frequency of the moment. One moment can play off of another and use more or less energy depending on the situation, which changes its frequency.

Using too much energy all of the time can make you feel drained and tired. This is especially true if you're around negative situations or people. It takes more energy to deal with negativity because it's a lower vibration that can pull your own frequency down to its level. If you're trying to be more balanced, then avoiding negativity is a great place to start because your frequency will no longer fluctuate as much. When it's flowing in an even manner it's easier for you to stay centered and balanced.

Emotions also affect the frequency of a moment. If you're happy, the frequency of the moment elevates and has a positive effect on you. If you're angry or upset, then the frequency in that moment can lower, become darker, and have a negative effect on you. Negative energy has a tendency to hang around, making you rethink the situation over and over again while coming up with *I should have said...* scenarios. If you find yourself replaying an encounter with someone repeatedly, then find a way to balance the situation within yourself. There's nothing you can do to change it now, and releasing the negativity will make you feel better then stewing over the situation.

Accept it as a learning experience and let it go. Another way the frequency of a moment can affect you is when you hold your emotions about the moment inside instead of releasing them. It doesn't matter if the emotions are positive or negative, that energy has to be released in some way. If you don't like expressing your emotions by talking about them you could try writing them down in a journal or a diary. Exercising can also help you express your emotions. Walking with a spring in your step when you're happy or power walking when you're mad helps to work off the excess energy and gives you time to think about the situation that made you happy or mad in the first place. By the time you've finished your walk, you'll often find you've worked off the energy and come to a solution to a problem or thought of something else you can do that will make you happy. Without the weight of emotions that have been held in too long, you'll feel lighter, more carefree, and in balance. It's always good to find a way to handle the things in life that bother you and cause you stress than it is to hold them inside where they can fester.

Finding the frequency of a moment can help you feel the energy as it surrounds you. To do this, pick a particular moment to analyze. Perhaps you're sitting at your desk working and suddenly decide to feel the frequency of that moment. Consider how the energy flows around you, how it affects you, and what you're feeling. The more you do this the

Chapter Four

more connected you'll be to the frequency of the moments of your life.

Try It Now Exercise:
WHAT CAN YOU RELEASE TODAY?

In order to allow new things to enter your life, there has to be room for them. Every new thing we want to do, or every new person we want to be involved with, requires our time and energy. If you have too many things going on in your life then you'll eventually get to the point where nothing else will fit. This is when you have to decide what is working for you, what you want to keep doing, and what needs to go. If something is no longer serving your best interest, if it is negative or draining to your energy, then it might be time to release it. Letting go of the negative will lighten and raise your frequency. It gives you clarity of purpose and is often the beginning of a spiritual awakening. When you begin questioning if something is serving a purpose in your life or holding you back from living your life's purpose, the truth will resonate within you. Deep inside, you'll intuitively know what you need to release even if it's something you think you want to keep.

As you begin to consider what you can release today, you'll need to evaluate the things happening in your life. Making a list and separating it into various categories will help you see what you need to let go.

Start by looking at the things you do each day. Write down what you do from the time you wake up until you go to bed for one entire day. As you consider what you've written, decide if there are activities you are doing that someone else could do just as well. If there are chores or other things you could delegate to lighten your load, that's one way to let go.

Now look at your relationships. Think about the dynamics of the relationship. If it's a relationship that you're definitely not going to let go of, are there any issues in the relationship that could be dealt with and parts of it released so you're both feeling more at ease? For instance, if you're constantly arguing with someone over something that, in the grand scheme of things, isn't going to make a big difference in your lives, then try to pick your battles. Is it something you can ignore or just deal with to eliminate an argument? Can you make your reasons why it bothers you so much clearer to the other person so they can also try to make an effort to deal with it, change it, or ignore it? Compromise is at the basis of every relationship but it has to come from both parties or the relationship doesn't work. It's a give-and-take situation and only you know how much you're willing to give and how much you can take before you've had enough. Some relationships you may be willing to let go. If there is someone you've befriended at work but who is constantly stirring up drama, which bothers or upsets you, then spending less time with them might be the best route to take. Some people you may end up cutting out of your life completely. In the end, only you know what is working for you and what isn't when it comes to your relationships. I'm all for second chances and working out problems, but we also have to remember that we can't change anyone else either. The desire to change has to come from deep within them before it will transform into the changes actually being made.

Next, you'll make a list of where you see your life going in the next five years. Look back at the previous two lists to see if

Chapter Four

anything on those lists are things you plan to still be doing at that time. If they are, then those are things you need to hold on to. If not, then those are the things you might need to release.

Chapter Five
BECOME MORE MINDFUL

Mindfulness is an important element for creating a cozy life for yourself. When you're mindful of what you're doing and what's happening around you, then you can take specific actions to bring more coziness into your life. Mindfulness has been around for thousands of years and has helped millions of people create positive influences in their lives. It can also help you to determine how you can increase the amount of coziness you're experiencing through being mindful and attentive of all aspects of your life.

WHAT IS MINDFULNESS?

Mindfulness means actively paying attention to what is happening in the present moment by attuning to that moment without judging it as good or bad, right or wrong. It is living your life with purpose, knowing each moment really matters, and actually noticing what is happening to you and around you. Mindfulness is an awareness of every sensation you feel and every thought and emotion you have, and then accepting them as your truth without criticism. When you're practicing

Chapter Five

mindfulness, you're fully focused on the here and now, the moment you're living right this minute, instead of dwelling on things that happened yesterday or imagining what might happen tomorrow, much like fika in Sweden (see chapter 1).

Originating in the Buddhist religion more than 2,600 years ago, Buddha gave his monks the responsibility of teaching others about the Four Foundations of Mindfulness, which are mindfulness of the body, mind, feelings, and phenomena (*dhammas*) in order to know each of these as they really are. Mindfulness is now practiced all over the world because of the benefits it gives you on both a personal and spiritual level. The concept of mindfulness was brought to the United States in 1979 by Jon Kabat-Zinn, Professor of Medicine Emeritus at the University of Massachusetts Medical School. He created the Stress Reduction Clinic and the Center for Mindfulness in Medicine, Health Care, and Society. His system originally contained the Buddhist philosophy, but he later removed those teachings and renamed the program Mindfulness-Based Stress Reduction (MBSR) in order to move mindfulness into the realms of science so it would become a clinical practice, which it has.

Since we aren't automatically mindful, we have to teach ourselves to be. Typically, we're off and running, doing this and that, and breezing through our lives, which often means we're missing a lot that's happening around us, and to us, simply because we're not paying attention. Mindfulness keeps us focused on the task at hand instead of worrying about how other people are completing the same task or if we're doing it right or wrong. It can help us keep an open mind about everything. When you're mindful, you don't pass judgment.

You listen, understand, and know the experience is worthwhile. You don't judge others for their decisions because it is their path, not your own. Mindfulness will change you, transforming your perception of the world and the way you act and react to other people. It also changes the way you perceive yourself and your place within the Divine. Mindfulness teaches you to observe instead of reacting, to remain calm instead of losing your temper, and to create effective reactions to the situations you find yourself involved in instead of responding blindly based on emotion. Mindfulness broadens your horizons, expands your mind, and gives you profound insights into spirituality.

Within the Buddhist tradition, mindfulness is practiced through meditation and breathing techniques that are done while sitting on the floor in the customary lotus position. However, many people also practice mindfulness while going about their day, without taking the time to do a traditional meditation ritual. Sometimes you just don't have the time to sit and meditate but you still want to make mindfulness a big part of your day. I enjoy doing five-minute meditations while sitting at my desk or at other times throughout my day to help me focus on being mindful.

THE ENERGY OF SELF-AWARENESS

Self-awareness means you know what your feelings are, what drives you, and the things you want out of life. You know your gifts and faults, the areas where you need to make changes or improvements in your life, your attitude, and your outlook. It means you're mindful of yourself on many levels. The energy that surrounds being self-aware is part of your frequency. If

Chapter Five

this gets out of balance, then you'll need to take steps to restore it by becoming more self-aware. The more you understand your inner self the more you'll understand what is causing your actions and reactions.

Becoming more self-aware may not fix every problem you have, but it's a great place to start. The better you know yourself, the more information you have at your disposal to make decisions. For instance, if you know you're afraid of heights, then you're not going to look over the edge of a tall building, are you? If you're aware that you tend to talk too much, then you can make a concentrated effort to streamline what you're saying and not dominate a conversation. It's difficult to make changes like this, especially if you're an outgoing, chatty person. But if you try, that's what matters.

As you practice being more aware of the energy of yourself, think about this. When you were created in the spiritual realm, you were perfection, which will never change. When you are born into the earthly realm, you're still the same perfect energy that you are in the spiritual realm but now you have to deal with a physical body that offers its own unique set of challenges. It's a huge learning curve, but that's the purpose of living in the physical realm—to learn. You'll always be you whether you're in the spiritual realm or the earthly plane of existence. Being self-aware in the physical realm really helps you connect to your spiritual self because you look deeper, feel more, and understand yourself more. When you can see yourself as a miracle of creation and appreciate that there is no one else exactly like you on either the physical or spiritual planes, then you will love yourself more, feel more joy, and be able to share your uniqueness of spirit unconditionally with others.

Understanding the energy of self-awareness means striving to learn as much as possible in order to grow in spirit while on the earthly plane. It's accepting all of the flaws of our physical body, discovering and relearning about our spiritual self, and learning how to treat others as we would on the spiritual plane. The energy of self-awareness is always positive and in forward motion; it's up to us to move forward with it.

MINDFULNESS AND PERSONAL GROWTH

Many of us, myself included, can get so busy that we move through life too quickly and things happening around us can become a blur. When this happens to me, I have to step on the brakes, slow myself down, and purposefully make mindfulness a priority. I want to enjoy the little things in life, like connecting with the dragonfly who got stuck in the rain the other day and couldn't move because he was wet. I put him in the barn to dry out and, after a while, he flew away. If I hadn't been mindful, I would have missed that he flew right by me. Being attuned to physical sensations, like the rain on my skin and his little feet as he stepped onto my finger, made me feel more mindful and appreciative of both the rain and the dragonfly.

Practicing mindfulness can bring about great changes in your perspective which leads to person growth. It creates a need within you to slow down and relax, to notice more and be more aware of everything. It helps you to realize that everything changes from one moment to the next. If you're holding onto a set way of thinking you might find yourself considering things outside of what you perceive as the only

Chapter Five

way to do something. When you let go of preconceived notions it opens the door to allow you to consider other options which can lead to more spontaneity, which helps you grow and learn about new things. Mindfulness can help you become more aware, less stressed, and happier overall.

Mindfulness can help you overcome behaviors that are obsessive, negative, and self-depreciating. When you are more mindful, it's easier to see where you're making the same mistakes over and over again. Once you realize what you're doing then you can take the steps necessary to change that behavior. For instance, if you get aggravated at checkout clerks who take a long time to ring up people's items, then you will assume that the situation is causing your annoyance. But if you're mindful about it, you will recognize that your irritation isn't at the clerk but it has become a habit because you always want to do things quickly and this person is slowing you down. Instead of letting yourself get mad, work through the emotion, allowing yourself to break the pattern of negativity so you remain calm. Noticing your behaviors in this way enables you to make changes within your own energy, which can raise your vibration and allow you to move forward in your personal growth. Over time, you'll find that you lose your temper less often when you practice mindfulness because you can stop your negative reactions, which can lower your frequency, from happening.

Personal growth through mindfulness means you're able to learn from your new awareness and apply what you're learning to your life. Becoming more aware can also lead you to being more easily distracted because now you're taking the time to be present in the moment and you'll notice things you've never paid attention to before. This will happen more at the beginning of your mindfulness journey. As you become accustomed to being mindful you'll still be distracted but you'll be more attuned to your inner self and it will be easier to bring your attention back to where you want it to be.

DEVELOP A CALM CONCENTRATION

One of the most common ways to develop a calm concentration while practicing mindfulness is to become aware of your breathing; feeling the air move in and out of your body, focusing on just that one thing and nothing else. As you breathe you may have a thought or feeling enter your mind. Address it or dismiss it and then return your focus to your breathing. If you don't want to focus on your breathing, you could become aware of the sensations you're feeling in your physical body or the sounds you're hearing around you. Focus on what feels right for you.

Keeping your focus on one specific thing allows for a deeper calmness to come over you as you're working on mindfulness. When you're experiencing this level of focus and concentration, you are able to observe your thoughts and feelings without being emotionally attached to them, you're not judgmental, and you're able to see your specific intentions. Imagine yourself as a spiritual being surrounded in darkness. Then you see a thought appear in the darkness that looks like orange words just moving across a black screen. Your spirit sees the thought, acknowledges what it means, but continues with the calm, focused, mindful meditation. The fact that you acknowledged the thought is a moment of mindfulness.

Chapter Five

Developing a calm concentration while practicing mindfulness can help you in other areas of your life because you'll tend to carry this feeling with you even when you're no longer meditating. Mindfulness helps reduce stress; increase our ability to learn, focus, and remember; tune out distractions; and become more empathetic. You'll feel more positive and optimistic about life; instead of being so hard on yourself, you'll give yourself a break now and then, and you'll find that you're less angry, frustrated, or annoyed.

Have you ever become overly aware of how a word sounds? So much so that when you say the word it no longer makes sense? Try saying the word *tongue* over and over and over out loud until it gets to the point that it no longer describes anything but is simply an odd-sounding word. This is a way that a calm concentration can manifest into überawareness. You're so aware of the word that it disassociates from its meaning.

One way that I like to work on having a calm but deep concentration is to pause in between movements to see what I feel. For example, when walking out to the barn I'll often stop halfway just to listen to the sounds of the horses, the highway, and the birds. This helps to embrace the energy of these sounds, which is refreshing after spending hours writing at the computer. You might pause as you get into your car to feel the door handle and smell the scent of the interior.

Another way you can connect to the calm concentration of mindfulness is to enjoy the things you do more. Instead of scarfing down a piece of toast and hot coffee as you're running out the door to work, get up earlier and sit down and smell the coffee as you drink it, feel the crunch of the toast as you eat it, and walk out of your house with purpose and awareness of the day waiting for you outside.

BEING REFLECTIVE TO BRING ABOUT CHANGE

Life is all about change. It happens whether you want it to or not. It's often easier to make the change yourself than it is to continue along your current path, until something happens that changes your life for you, maybe even in a way you prefer it hadn't changed. Sometimes we can get so caught up in things that aren't in our best interest that we can't see we're heading down a path of self-destruction. Taking the time to be reflective about your life and the path you're on, seriously considering how you live and how you want to live can help you see the things you're doing that you need to change to get back in balance. Once you have a clear vision of what you want to change, you can create a plan that will enable you to achieve those goals.

Change has to begin within you. No one else can do it for you. There has to be a desire within your spirit that is pulling you in the right direction. Your higher self may be sending you messages in your dreams to let you know you're heading in the wrong direction, or maybe you've been given a second chance at life. Reflect on the things that have happened to you and make yourself aware of the times you've been given a second chance or the support from another so you can change negatives to positives. If you're feeling negative about yourself as a person— that you're undeserving, or don't feel love for yourself—then these feelings should be addressed so you recognize you're a wonderful person who deserves everything the universe has to offer. You are worthy of all you can achieve

Chapter Five

because you have incarnated on Earth. Another person's opinions of you may be important to you, but the amount of love you feel for yourself doesn't rely on living up to their expectations of you. What is right for them may not be right for you. Try not to let someone else's negativity affect how much you love yourself.

As you experience quiet reflection and then make changes in your life based on what you discovered about yourself during that time of reflection, work internally to sort through any emotions you have about the things you do that you want to change. For instance, if you've been mean to someone because you just don't like them, instead try to treat them nicely. Or dig deeper to figure out exactly why you don't like the person and address those reasons. Work internally to forgive past wrongs if necessary and address any issues of guilt or whatever feelings are causing you to act outside of your normal character to someone else. If you find it difficult to be responsible for your actions or to instigate change through reflection, then take the time to look deeper still and to be honest with yourself about yourself. Admitting you've made wrong choices or that change needs to happen so you can feel happy again can be a hard thing to do, but it's a step toward healing and a step toward positive change.

We are each responsible for ourselves. When we bring about changes within our lives then we're acting on our responsibilities. When life seems chaotic, take some time to regroup, analyze, and evaluate so you can find your way back to a balanced, cozy, stress-free life.

FINDING BALANCE IN YOUR SPIRITUALITY

Being in balance means that physically and spiritually you're moving along in joy, peacefulness, and without worry or stress. Being in tune with your spiritual self is essential to being in spiritual balance. To understand yourself better, think about what inspires you at a soul level, what is most important to you in this lifetime, and what challenges, inspires, motivates, and guides you along your life path. Think about your gifts and talents that make you unique. Consider your levels of awareness about different aspects of your spirituality. Are you in tune with your intuition, letting it guide you, or do you ignore impressions you receive?

When you're in spiritual balance life flows easily, when you're out of balance it doesn't. You may have a niggling feeling that something isn't quite right but you just can't put your finger on what it is.

Realizing that you will experience times of balance and being out of balance all through your life will help you to recognize when it's happening so you can find the cause and bring yourself back to center. Moments of recognition of your spiritual truths can shine new light on your beliefs. Living with passion, focus, and joy goes a long way to staying in balance. Understanding your soul's purpose and continually growing in spirit will help you follow your divine plan with all of its ups and downs.

Chapter Five

Try It Now Exercise:
A Working Meditation

Meditation is a great way to obtain balance in your life. In this chapter, since we're talking about balance, I'd like to introduce you to a form of meditation that is often called a working meditation. The reason for this name is because it is a meditation that happens when you're working on something else. It's easy to fall into a meditative state when doing mundane or repetitive tasks. Part of your mind is on the work you're doing but your thoughts wander elsewhere. I've often discovered that I get my best ideas during working meditations.

Let me give you an example of a working meditation. The stalls in our barn have to be cleaned twice daily. Picking up horse manure isn't exactly fun or glamorous work, but it can be calming. So imagine this—you're cleaning stalls and there's a breeze blowing through the barn. The scent of the hay carries on the breeze. If you're cleaning the turnouts, then the sun warms your skin. You hear the chewing, breathing, snorting, and sometimes a nicker while you're doing your work. A horse nuzzles you, so you take a few moments to rub it. While you're doing this, your mind is taking in your surroundings, but it is also wandering. In my case, I often wonder about what type of book I should write next or I go over the pros and cons of an idea or sometimes I just relax into that meditative state and release any negative emotions I might have. For me, there's just something about being around horses that can erase a bad mood, anger, or any other negative emotion and replace it with a sense of calmness and balance. So while I'm working in the barn, my mind calms, which makes it easier to make decisions I have been contemplating.

You can experience the same type of working meditation if you're washing your car, doing laundry, cleaning your house, washing dishes by hand, playing golf, or coming up with a creative repair like they do in India when practicing jugaad (see chapter 1). Anytime you're engaged in an activity where you don't have to be completely attentive and actively engaged in what you're doing, then there is the possibility of turning it into a working meditation session. If you've got a situation that you can't get off your mind, then contemplate it while you're sweeping and mopping the floor. Or if you need a new idea for a project at work, are making a major life decision, or need to weigh the pros and cons of something, then do it while you're cutting the grass.

A working meditation can help you reduce levels of stress and anxiety. It improves your mood, boosts your creativity, assists in decision-making, and helps you come up with solutions to adverse situations. It makes you feel more optimistic, less negative, more focused, and empowered. Working meditations also help you solve problems, have brainstorming sessions within yourself, and help you process information in a more balanced way instead of approaching a situation only through your emotions.

If you wanted to do a working meditation during your walk, I'd suggest slowing the pace down a bit. In other words, take a stroll instead of a power walk, look at your surroundings, appreciate the area in which you live, and let your mind tackle the issues bothering you. By the end of your stroll, you'll probably have reached a solution.

Chapter Five

CREATE MEANINGFUL RELATIONSHIPS THROUGH MINDFULNESS

Relationships are built upon a mutual trust between you and another person, whether it's a romantic interest, a professional colleague, or a friend. Trust must be authentic and real. Think about it—you're putting yourself in a position where the other person, should they choose to break that trust, could hurt you emotionally. Trust means you believe and are committed to your relationship with this person regardless of the consequences of their actions.

Mindfulness helps us create more meaningful relationships with other people because we are more aware of their feelings, we are optimistic about our interactions with them, and we are accepting of them in every way. There are no conditions on how we feel about them, which brings two people closer. Mindfulness in a relationship means we are present and active in our interaction with the other person; we're patient and honest with them, and we often go out of our way to do things for them. We truly listen to them by giving our undivided attention, we care about their opinions, and we enjoy their company. We are committed to interacting with this person. By being mindful in our relationships with others we let them know they matter to us, which is part of gemütlichkeit (see chapter 1).

When you practice mindfulness, you have a better understanding of yourself, which in turn helps you have a better understanding of other people. This enables you to have a better relationship with them. It's important to also understand that you should never have to sacrifice yourself, your beliefs, and what you want out of life, for someone else. One of our purposes in life is to be our true, authentic selves. If we suppress our true nature just to satisfy what someone else wants us to do, then we're not fulfilling our true purpose. Being mindful of ourselves, our purpose, and having respect for ourselves will help us to weed out those people in our lives who don't have our best interests at heart.

In every relationship, we expect certain things of the other person. We expect them to treat us kindly, to be there for us as we are for them, and to give us their trust and not break our trust in them by doing negative or unacceptable things in the relationship. For example, you don't expect your significant other to hurt you by cheating on you with someone else. If they do, that is often a game changer. Sometimes our expectations can be way too high, which makes it difficult for the other person to be able to meet them. When that happens, we're disappointed and upset. If you keep your expectations reasonable for the relationship, then you'll run less of a risk of being disappointed and may even be surprised more often.

During our lifetimes, we will have hundreds of relationships with people of all walks of life, not just romantic relationships. Every relationship we develop will teach us something about ourselves, will help us grow through those lessons, and will make us mindfully aware for future relationships. Each one also teaches us something about other people, how they act and react, which helps us decide what types of behaviors are acceptable or unacceptable to us. As we walk our paths and try our best to be true to our individual spiritual self, mindfulness will help us build strong relationships that have long-term staying power.

Chapter Five

PAUSE AND REFLECT TO CHANGE DIRECTIONS

Have you ever been going in one direction and then suddenly gotten a really strong urge to turn around and go in a completely other direction? I've had this happen to me when I was driving only to later find out that there was a car accident down the road from the original direction I was traveling. Intuition can compel us to make drastic changes like this, 180-degree turnarounds, for apparently unknown reasons, especially if we're being protected in some way. Mindfulness can also cause you to change directions completely if you'll only pause to reflect on your path.

If you're not sure what you want out of life, practicing mindfulness can help you gain clarity. As you become more aware and clear through mindfulness about what you want to accomplish in your life, you may realize you have to go in the completely opposite direction from where you're currently headed. If this is the case, you can start to make small changes to achieve the new life you want so the change is gradual instead of a drastic deviation in a different direction. If you're unhappy in your job or if you want to make personal changes but can't seem to stick to what you have to do to make the change, small mindful steps will help you achieve results. For instance, if you want to lose some weight you don't just stop eating. Instead, you make mindful healthy choices to improve your diet and result in weight loss. If the job isn't making you happy, then you take small mindful steps to improve your work situation, but if that doesn't work you could take classes in the field you want to work in or start looking for another position instead of quitting your job before you have something else lined up.

To mindfully make the decision to go in a different direction, it helps to pause and reflect on where you are, why you're no longer happy in your current situation, and the steps needed to make the change. Once you've considered all of these things, then make a commitment to yourself to see your decision through until you've achieved your goals. Along the path make sure you continue to pause and reflect on your progress. Consider how far you've come and be proud of yourself. Giving yourself a pat on the back for a job well done keeps your self-esteem high and your motivation going strong.

Changing directions in your life can sometimes feel like the rug has been pulled out from under your feet, especially if it's a change that is out of your hands or you weren't anticipating. During these types of situations, mindfulness can play a key role in getting you back on track, keeping a positive attitude, and maintaining forward motion. If you feel like you're getting overwhelmed by too much change happening too quickly, pausing to simply breathe while attuning to your awareness, your intention, and your attitude about the situation can help to ground you so that you can regain your balance. Once you feel focused again, you can face the situation in a mindful manner. Mindfulness will help you keep your emotions in check instead of letting them get out of control, it enables you to see what needs to be done right now, in the moment, so you can meet the changes happening with a smile on your face and contentment inside yourself. You know there is purpose in everything and you'll come through it just fine.

Chapter Five

Try It Now Exercise:
MAKE A MOVING TOWARD COZY PROJECT

To find balance in life through mindfulness and to live in coziness and simplicity, there will be times when you have to make changes. For this exercise, you'll be creating an outline of different areas of your life where you'd like to make mindful changes. I'm going to give you some topic ideas to get you started.

When I did this project for myself, I bought a small journal for my outline. In the beginning part of it, I spent some time mindfully thinking about what I wanted to change and I wrote it all down in the journal. Then in the pages after the outline, I kept a journal for six months and wrote about my progress and whether or not I was meeting my goals. During this process, you'll discover that alternate ideas will come to you when something isn't working. Make note of these ideas and try them out. If one thing doesn't work, then something else just might be the perfect solution to the change you want to make. I would suggest that you do this project for a minimum of one month. Or you can just work on it until you've made all of the changes a permanent part of your life, regardless of how long it takes.

Within my project, some of the areas I wanted to work on were the following: find balance between writing and running our other businesses, letting go of what no longer serves me, spending more time with family and friends, creating a deeper connection to my spiritual self, make my home cozier by discarding or donating things that I no longer need, spend more time outside, move more, take better care of myself, appreciate everyone (including myself) more, do nice things for people I don't know, and to find time to slow down and just be me. Feel free to use some of these for your own project or come up with additional ones for yourself. Also, you can create subheadings within your main topic headers to refine your changes. For instance, under my header of discarding or donating I made a list of all of the rooms in the house, then as I completed the room I checked it off the list.

Some of the things you'll include in the project will be ones you'll want to do for the rest of your life. Interweave these into your daily life so that they become a permanent part of who you are.

OVERCOMING OBSTACLES TO MINDFULNESS

As with any endeavor, there will be times when you'll feel like there are too many obstacles in your path to keep pursuing your goal. And, as with any endeavor, if you want to be successful, you have to overcome those obstacles. Let's take a look at some of the obstacles you might encounter as you're practicing mindfulness.

When I started learning about mindfulness, I thought you had to sit in the lotus position and say *om* in order to be successful. After a few attempts, I decided that I just didn't have the time to do that. So I forgot about it completely. Fast-forward a few years and mindfulness reappears in my life. This time I tried a different method and took a few minutes at various times of the day to be more aware and mindful of what was going on around me and to quiet my mind at the same time. I imagined everything happening in slow motion when my awareness was engaged. This worked for me to help me overcome the obstacle of not having enough time.

Chapter Five

Focusing on the negative instead of the positive when you're being mindful happens sometimes. It's hard to push negative thoughts away and focus on your breathing when you're in the middle of a difficult situation. When this happens to me, I tell myself that I deserve a temporary reprieve from worrying about the situation, and I use creative visualization to make a big steel box in my mind that has a key to lock it. Then I put all of my thoughts about the situation into that box and lock them up. Now, I get some time to just think about myself and to focus on being more centered and balanced in my life, which ultimately will help me deal with what's in that locked box. When I feel ready, I'll unlock the box and let the situation out. Since I practice mindfulness in short sessions throughout the day, I sometimes leave that stuff in there for hours until I decide to go back to it. Giving yourself a break can be rejuvenating.

Being mindful requires an ongoing effort. It's really easy to forget to be mindful when you're distracted by other things happening in your life. For me, catalysts to be more mindful are negative emotions like irritation and anger. When I feel those emotions rising, I automatically focus and become more mindful about the situation. That doesn't mean I never blow up, but it does mean that it takes a whole heck of a lot to get me to that point. As you're practicing mindfulness, you might discover you also have catalysts that will cause you to become more mindful.

Distractions, especially if you're a person who is easily distracted, can have you giving up before you realize it. It's very easy to say you'll get back to practicing mindfulness later because right now you have to walk the dog or whatever thing has come up that is distracting you. Try giving yourself just five minutes at a time to focus and become more aware. Doing mindfulness work while you're in the shower is a great way to achieve this! When you practice in small amounts of time, there is less time for you to get distracted and you will not want to quit.

LETTING YOUR MIND WANDER

When practicing mindfulness you first quiet your mind, and focus on your breathing before becoming mindfully aware. Runners do this every time they go for a run, even if they don't realize it. There's something about hearing your feet hit the ground or pavement, feeling each breath you take that silences that chatterbox in your head. Physical activity that works your muscles, makes you sweat, and clears your mind enables you to connect to mindfulness.

Letting your mind wander will help you be more open minded and understanding to other people if you give your mind the task of considering how other people feel about things or what they might be thinking. Considering what they're going through can help you feel more connected to them at a soul level.

Letting your mind wander is also another way to become more mindful, to feel more spiritual coziness and it can also help you become more creative. To me it feels like your mind is plugged into the creativity of the Universe and the ideas become plentiful. And because you're being mindful, you can pick and choose the idea that feels right for you. I've always said I get my best ideas when I'm cleaning a stall or grooming a horse. It's because my mind is quiet, I'm connected to spiritual energy of coziness within the barn, and I pay attention to words, ideas, and images that randomly pop into my mind. Sometimes the inspiration is one word, other times I see it as a scene playing out in my mind's eye.

When your mind wanders it can come up with some wonderful fantastical stories. Talk about being creative! Have you ever noticed that if you have a problem and you stop thinking about it but instead you just zone out for a few minutes that all of a sudden the answer to the problem pops into your head? This is the energy of mindfulness helping you out. While you're zoned out, you have to be mindfully aware in order to pay enough attention to receive the answer you're given so that you remember it and put it to work for you.

Feeling zoned out, spaced out, or in la-la land are just ways that our body shuts down our brains to give us a rest for a moment. If you're overly tired you'll have it happen more than when you're well rested. It's the brain's way of practicing a bit of mindfulness on its own. When it slows you down like this, you can be aware of things that are happening when your mind is in this state. Then again, if you're exhausted you just might go to sleep.

Anytime you have the opportunity to daydream or let your mind wander, you'll feel a connection to mindfulness and spiritual coziness. It's what you do with the information you receive during your wandering that is important. If you obtain information that helps you notice something that will specifically help you or someone else, or if you realize you know how to do something now that was giving you difficulty before, then you've found answers on a spiritual level.

Letting your mind wander has many benefits. Try it today and see what kind of great things you can discover about yourself, the world you live in, and those who share it with you.

ATTENTION TO DETAILS

Do you pay attention to details? I'm a very detail-oriented person, sometimes too much so. I notice little things like if someone got a new mailbox or if a house got painted or if someone cut down a tree. Just little changes in my environment that no one else notices until I say *oh look*. I also notice a lot of other little details, like what people are wearing, misspelled words, missing punctuation, patterns, price changes, and when items have been physically moved to a different place. If you've ever entered a room that no one was supposed to be in while you were gone and just knew that someone had been inside—that's paying attention to the details of the energy of the room. You're sensing the energy disturbance from another person's energy entering into your space.

As you're learning to be more mindful, paying attention to details is part of the process. When you notice the small things like an ant crawling across the leaf of a daisy or the way rain runs off the tip of the leaf, then you're being mindful and aware of those things. In Japan, they practice wabi-sabi (see chapter 1), where beauty is found in the imperfections of age and wear. Imperfections are a small thing to notice but can reveal a lot about an item. When you're focused at a deeper level, you're noticing the little things instead of just looking at the big picture.

Chapter Five

Paying attention to details is important in our everyday lives. When you're mindful about the specifics then you'll make fewer errors, which gives you a higher level of accuracy in your work. Noticing details can help you make a good impression, which is especially helpful if you're applying for a new job or trying to get a raise or a promotion at work. What if you're house hunting? Noticing the details can help you get the best price possible on the house and save you from having to spend more on repairs in the long run. Paying attention to details helps keep you safer. You're not going to step out in front of a moving car if you're paying attention to where you're going and looking both ways before crossing the street. If you're an accountant, you have to pay attention to the numbers you're dealing with in order to be accurate in your work.

Paying attention to details about yourself is also an important aspect of mindfulness. We always tend to take care of others before we take care of ourselves. Pay attention to how you're feeling, your vision, your teeth, the kind of shape you're in physically and if you need to make changes, then start a plan to do so. In addition, be aware of the details of your emotions. If you're feeling out of sorts, do a traditional meditation session for mindfulness to look for the reason you're not at 100 percent.

Life is in the details; notice them to feel more joy, abundance, and coziness.

Mindfulness Is Nonjudgmental

Being judgmental means you're quick to have an excessively critical and negative perspective about someone, including yourself, or about a situation, that can block your spiritual growth, keep you from being more mindful, and cause problems for you in your daily life. Mindfulness discourages having a judgmental point of view. Think about the emotions underlying judgmental feelings. Emotions are always trying to tell us something, so it's important not to suppress them but to acknowledge and work through them.

How do you recognize when a thought is judgmental or not? Is it negative, accusatory, or condemning? Then it's probably judgmental. Let's look at society for a second. Think about television shows, social media, or product advertisements. How many times have you compared yourself to people in society who are famous, rich, or embody some quality you would like to have for yourself? When you compare yourself and say things like, *I'll never have that much money, I can't wear my hair like her*, or *I want to be famous like him but I don't think I'll ever make it*. All of these are judgmental thoughts because you're judging yourself against what someone else is doing. When practicing mindfulness, it's just as important to not judge yourself as it is to not judge other people.

When you find yourself having judgmental thoughts, remember this, each one of us is already divinely perfect at a soul level. It is our responsibility to one another to try to understand each other instead of being judgmental to one another. There is so much hatred in the world that could be neutralized if we'd only see that we all are the same deep inside. We are all strong spiritual beings here to learn specific lessons. We must become aware of this in order to understand and accept that love and kindness is important to share with others while living on the earthly plane of existence. Try looking at situations from the perspective of the other people involved. Does it change how you see things? We are more accepting of ourselves and others as we are, with all of our flaws, because we are all the same.

Being judgmental will not make you happy; it will make you upset and miserable, so why do it? If you are constantly judging yourself against someone else or if you're always thinking you can't do this or you'll never do that, you create a self-fulfilling prophecy. By being mindful, you will be aware of when these thoughts come up. This will give you the chance to not give judgmental thinking power over you. There is purpose in mindfulness.

Making Mindfulness a Priority

Giving mindfulness priority in your life is the best way to experience both personal and spiritual growth through awareness. Mindfulness awakens us to what we are really experiencing every single day. It gives us clarity of thought and purpose, which makes us happier. To reach the goal of being more mindful, you have to give the process of mindfulness a high priority in your life. And don't worry, it's not going to take up all of your time and you don't have to give it a high priority forever because soon it will become second nature for you. It's normally in the beginning stages to spend extra time on being mindful. Here are some ways to make practicing mindfulness a priority.

Pick a cozy, quiet place in your home where you can sit and practice. Get yourself a soft, round rug that you can sit on if you're doing a traditional meditation session or a favorite blanket that you can snuggle into while lounging in your comfy chair if you meditate in a casual way. You'll give mindfulness a higher priority if you have an area dedicated to meditating and mindfulness work.

If you need more structure when it comes to practicing mindfulness, you might check your local community colleges to see if they offer classes on mindfulness. Attending a structured event with a teacher can help you get off on the right foot. You'll make new friends with a shared interest too.

Be kind and patient with yourself. When you make taking care of yourself a priority, it is easier to let mindfulness also be a priority. When you take care of yourself then you're in a better position to take care of others or to help out when needed.

Some of the ways you can make mindfulness a priority in your life is to take a morning or evening walk, do yoga, set aside time for meditation, spend time with yourself doing things you like to do, spend time in nature, or go for a swim. Any situation where you can be active and clear and quiet your mind will help you connect to mindfulness by focusing inside of yourself to connect to your spiritual essence, universal consciousness, or simply to let your mind notice the simple things in life. Staring out of the passenger window on a car drive, watching the scenery go by in a way to tune into mindfulness.

When you make mindfulness a priority, it can help you heal. If you've experienced a difficult situation or if you've recently broken up with someone or lost your job, being mindful and examining the situation through mindfulness, can give you insights as to why the situation unfolded the way it did. When you make mindfulness a priority and take the time to look at the situation in a mindful manner, sometimes you

Chapter Five

may even glean information you never would have considered if you hadn't used mindfulness as a tool to help you deal with the problem. The process of healing can cause you to feel emotions you'd rather leave buried. Mindfulness can help you to heal your heart over time.

Increasing your awareness is the primary goal of mindfulness. Making it a priority in your life will allow you to become more aware of yourself on many levels, of the people around you, and of the world you live in. With so much to learn through mindfulness, there's no wondering why it's become so popular.

Try It Now Exercise:
Journaling/Coloring

This is a two-part exercise. First, we'll look at journaling, and then let's get out the colored pencils and crayons!

Getting into the habit of journaling can help you keep track of the progress you're making while you're practicing mindfulness. Being in the moment, being more aware, and noticing the small things as well as the big picture are all aspects of mindfulness. Writing down the things you notice is a mindful activity. The more you write, the more you will notice and the more you notice, the more you will write. Mindful journaling helps you feel more present in your life, helps increase your awareness, and helps you see areas where you can practice being more mindful.

As you write in your mindfulness journal, try to include as many details about your observations as possible. Include what you see, the smell of the air around you, what something felt like, the sounds you heard, and what something tasted like.

Adjectives are your best friend when writing about what your senses felt. Being descriptive in your writing allows you to feel more present and in the moment, even if the moment was earlier in the day. It also helps you to get back into that same mindful place and the feelings you felt when you give full complete descriptions in your journal. Entries in your mindfulness journal can help you in the future to deepen your connection to mindful living.

Coloring for adults has really blossomed over the past couple of years. I've always loved to color, even when it wasn't a popular thing for adults to do, because it helps you focus and is just a lot of fun. Today, the coloring books for adults are marketed to help you become more mindful, to ease stress, and to relax. They have thicker paper than kids' coloring books and you could even frame your creations if you so desire. Looking at them after you've finished is a mindful practice. So head to your closest retailer, grab a coloring book that appeals to you, and get a box of colored pencils or crayons. Get a big box with a wide variety of colors so you have a lot of colors to choose from. Back at home, find a place where you can get comfortable, where it's quiet, and choose a picture from the book. You might decide to go from page one to the end or just pick pictures at random throughout the book. Now start to color and notice what happens.

As you color, you'll notice that your breathing slows down, you get more relaxed, and you feel calmer and more in tune with your inner self. Your mind starts to get quiet and the chatterbox that is usually talking a mile a minute shuts up (except to suggest a color choice here and there). Coloring engages your imagination, boosts your mindfulness, and

Chapter Five

increases your creativity. You'll end up with a wonderful picture too. Date each one somewhere on the page or on the back with a note or two for yourself, that way when you look back at them, you'll remember the coloring session and how you felt in that moment.

Chapter Six
SPEND TIME IN THE NATURAL WORLD

Spending time in the natural world, experiencing its beauty, peacefulness, power, and sacredness will help you to increase the amount of coziness you experience on a daily basis. Being outside is good for the soul. It brings you back to your spiritual roots and makes you feel part of a much bigger world and an even greater universe. It helps you to open your eyes to things you may have avoided or been blind to before. Make time to become cozy in nature and bring those feelings back with you when you return to your home. In this chapter, we'll discuss the importance of reconnecting with nature and how it relates to finding that sense of coziness. As a reminder, Shinrin-yoku, the practice of forest bathing in Japan, is one form of this kind of practice. Other coziness practices in nature include friluftsliv in Norway and uitwaaien in the Netherlands (see chapter 1).

CONNECT WITH NATURE

Connecting with nature is essential to living a cozy life. The more you can appreciate the world you live in, the simplicity

Chapter Six

yet complexity of the forests, mountains, oceans, and other ecosystems around the world, the more in tune you'll be with your reality on the earthly plane of existence. Because we are intrinsically part of nature itself, it only makes sense that it connects deeply with us on a soul level. When we can get in tune with nature, we can get more in tune with ourselves.

Going outside and doing activities in nature is a choice that only you can make. Some people love the outdoors and spend as much time outside as possible. Other people prefer staying inside. Even if you're the inside type, finding some time to be outside (other than walking to and from your car) will be advantageous to you. There are many benefits to being outside instead of staying stuck in the house day after day. Being outside improves our mental health and reduces our stress levels. There's just something about breathing in a deep breath of clean air that helps ground and center us. The negative ions in the air that are found in the mountains and around bodies of water help to calm us, making it easier to connect to our spiritual selves to balance and center our essential core essence. Being outside helps us let go of angry feelings and replace them with feelings of serenity. Doing activities in the sun gives us healthy doses of vitamin D (just make sure you're protecting your skin against the sun's harmful UV rays at the same time).

In the summer, if you enjoy running, swimming, or other outdoor activities, you'll find that doing them helps you feel more alive and more in tune with yourself. You'll also have a higher level of awareness of the world around you. If you're not accustomed to being outside, start with short periods of time and then work up to more. Short walks are a good way to get started. You might decide to plant a garden, do yoga outside, or visit a playground and swing on the swing set. To prevent falling into a routine that might become boring and easy to quit doing, change your activities from day to day. If you swim at the beach one day, then the next day go for a hike. Wintertime brings other exciting outside activities like skiing, snowshoeing, or ice skating. Do what you enjoy regardless of the season and you'll be able to make it a lifelong change.

While it's fun to do things outside with other people, to deepen your spiritual connection, make sure you do things in nature by yourself, just to spend time communing at a soul level with the feel of the wind on your face, as in the Dutch practice of uitwaaien (see chapter 1), the sand between your toes, the way the ocean breeze coats your skin with a layer of salt, or the way fog feels like a cool mist against your skin. When you're with other people, you'll often spend time talking and miss the little things about nature that provides for that deep, spiritual connection. Find a place to sit down and quietly become one with the natural world around you in mind, body, and spirit. As you sit there, let your mind empty of thoughts and ask your higher self to tell you things that you need to know about your spiritual path. Try not to ask about specific problems but instead ask for guidance on a larger scale. You can apply what you learn to the specific problems later.

RAINY DAYS

South Florida weather can change in the blink of an eye. Since I live in a tropical climate, it's not unusual for it to be pouring rain across the street and we're dry as can be. Some days we get a day long drizzle, which is nice, or sometimes it'll

Chapter Six

downpour for hours, and then everything floods. Some of us have to work in the rain, myself included, and sometimes getting drenched is good for the soul. Just make sure you're not outside in the middle of a lightning storm. Safety should always be your first priority.

Rain is essential for all life. It cleans everything, it gives the earth the moisture it needs so that plants can grow, and rainwater is still caught in many places around the world for drinking water. Doing something constructive on rainy days is a way to embrace cozy living and the joy found in doing something you've been putting off or spending time inside with family or friends. Rainy days are often times of great productivity, of immense relaxation by pampering yourself, or of trying something new. You might have people over for a hygge event of watching a movie marathon or to binge-watch a television show on demand.

Have you ever paid attention to the smell of the air after a rain shower or thunderstorm? It smells fresh and makes you feel calm and relaxed. The reason this happens is because the air is filled with negative ions, which have a positive effect on us. Negative ions can help relieve stress, boost our mood, feel more alert, and give us more energy. Negative ions are also found at the beach, in mountain mist, around waterfalls, and in the morning dew. That's why these places are often vacation destinations. They are relaxing, peaceful, and instill a sense of well-being within you because you're in the presence of negative ions. They are also known to purify the air, kill bacteria, and stimulate plant growth.

On the other hand, positive ions have the opposite effect and make you feel ill, grumpy, aggravated, and in a bad mood.

When earthquakes or other natural disasters happen, there are positive ions in the air prior to the event and the uneasy feelings that they cause make animals flee the areas before the event takes place. Electronics, like our computers and cell phones, produce positive ions. With the abundance of positive ions around us in our society, it's a good idea to expose yourself to negative ions routinely. You could get a negative ion generator for your home to help balance out the positive ions created by your electronic devices, computers, and televisions.

What kind of things can you do on a rainy day? In Norway, they practice koselig (see chapter 1), which is coziness without borders, so anything you do can add to the coziness in your life. A rainy day is a perfect time to enjoy a koselig day. When I was young, my favorite thing to do was stand in the yard and spin around, arms opened wide, and laugh in the rain. Sometimes I still do this. It's a great stress reliever. Other days, I cozy up with a blanket and a bowl of popcorn and watch a movie. Rainy days are great for relaxing or doing things you don't take the time to do on a regular basis. You can choose to be productive and get a lot of cleaning and organizing done in your house, or you can have a home spa day for yourself. Open a window and let the negative ions flood into your home to get an extra positive boost from nature itself.

GARDENING FOR THE MIND, BODY, AND SPIRIT

I grew up on a farm where every summer we planted a huge garden that consisted of tomatoes, potatoes, carrots, onions, strawberries, okra, watermelons, cantaloupes, cabbage, corn, sting beans, squash, lettuce, and butter beans. We had apple trees and grape vines, too. Some of my fondest memories are of

Chapter Six

making apple juice with a manual press, except for the yellow jackets, who also loved the apple juice–making process. As a kid on a farm, gardening was a fun way to pass the time, digging in the dirt and planting the seeds, tending the garden for weeds while feeling the sun on your back, and then harvesting the food.

Gardening is easy to do, is healthy for your body because you're moving, and helps to quiet your mind so you can contemplate things. Gardening calms you, brings a sense of peacefulness within even if you've had a very hectic day, and gives you something you can control, even if the rest of your life feels out of control. You'll be proud of your accomplishments in growing and tending to a garden. It's a living thing that needs your attention, and when you give it, the garden will flourish and you'll reap the benefits from your effort. You can also grow small indoor gardens of herbs and spices to add to the food you've grown and stored.

Not only does gardening help your mind, body, and spirit but it can also save you money when you freeze or can the food you grew. Organic food is expensive at the grocery store, so the savings can be considerable. Food you've grown yourself also had a richer taste than what you usually find in the store. Strawberries are a great example. When you grow your own strawberries, they'll be a vibrant red throughout, taste sweet, and, well, you could just eat them for days if you like strawberries. To find them like this in the store is a rare occurrence where I live. Usually the strawberry is white on the inside and red on the outside. This happens to many fruits and vegetables because they are harvested before they're really ripe so they don't spoil too quickly. Eating food you've grown also leads to a healthier diet and lifestyle.

Looking out over your garden from somewhere in your house or from your porch is oftentimes just as calming and relaxing as getting out there and digging in the dirt tending it. You get to watch the plants as they grow, to see a section of your yard change from what at first appears to be just bare dirt into an area flourishing with plant life. The natural beauty of a garden can brighten your mood, and it can give you a feeling of coziness and of being settled and grounded.

Creating a raised garden bed has also become popular. If you have back or knee issues, this could be the perfect way for you to still reap the benefits of gardening without putting stress on your knees and back. Whatever method you choose for your garden, you'll experience the mind, body, and spiritual benefits that come with planting, growing, and harvesting your own food. And if you have more than what you need, you could also donate it to others or sell it at the local farmer's market.

Bringing the Outside In

There's nothing quite like bringing the natural world inside your home. Not only does this add a tremendous amount of hominess and coziness to your life, but it connects you with the natural world without your having to leave the house. This is especially helpful in the winter months when it's difficult to move around outside due to inclement weather. There are so many ways you can bring the outside in that I honestly don't know where to start. So, I'll tell you some of my favorite ways to do it and let that be your starting point. Then you can turn

Chapter Six

on your creativity and find even more ways to create a natural atmosphere inside your home.

Bringing plants inside is a great way to add the natural world to your daily living space. Plants not only add oxygen to your home but they are lovely to look at, require minimal upkeep, and looking at them gives you a feeling of peacefulness.

If you like to collect things when on nature walks, you can create art with your findings and use them to decorate your home. Seashells, dried leaves, cool-looking pieces of wood, rocks, and any other items found in nature that you feel will make a good decoration for your individual space are great to use. The patterns, colors, and designs all add to the overall sense of coziness within your home. If you want to go for bigger items, large round stumps can be varnished and placed around your home so people can sit on them, you can bring a large tree inside, or, if you're constructing your home, build your home around the trees on your property. This gives your living space a one-of-a-kind flair. Or maybe you'd like to use a natural slab or rock for a sink or a bathtub made out of stone, wood, or even crystal. Granted a crystal bathtub is nearly a million dollars, but wouldn't that be cool to bathe in?

When you're decorating, consider using natural wood flooring or creating a wall out of stones and rocks. A staircase built around the trunk of an old tree adds a sense of coziness, uniqueness, and charm instead of just having a regular flight of stairs in the house. Using natural light by having lots of windows is a great way to bring the outside in as well. I think my favorite idea by far, though, is having a large skylight above your bed so you could fall asleep while looking at the night sky.

I can't tell you how many times, as a kid, I'd lie on a blanket in the yard at night while watching for shooting stars and end up falling asleep outside.

For the wall decorations, you might choose a variety of sizes of framed photographs. These can be as large as a wall or a small 3 x 5 image. Paintings on canvases also work. It's your preference as to which one you'd like to use. Or you could put paintings in one room and photography in another. Wallpaper that depicts images of the woods, the beach, or the mountains is a way to offer feelings of inspiration to anyone who looks at the wall. Photography is a wonderful way to show different areas around the world, to bring the peacefulness of the mountains or the beauty of the ocean into a location where you can view it daily, especially if you don't live near either place. Any way you can bring the outside in will help you live a cozier, calmer, and happier life.

The Energy of the Natural World

Energy exists all around us. It is in every person, place, and thing. It runs through the rivers and streams, it is in the air and part of the earth, sky, and stars. It exists in our galaxy and beyond. It is in the spiritual realm, in our minds, and part of our dreams. Energy is everywhere. To live in the coziness of the natural world, you have to be able to connect to its energy and feel it as a living presence. To do this you have to go outside, preferable to a forest, the beach, or somewhere that has a lot of plant life, where it is quiet and you can be alone. Then begin by noticing the little details in the natural area around you. What do you see? Are there boulders nearby? Do you feel compelled to sit on them? What do you hear? Maybe

Chapter Six

the babbling of a brook, the cry of a hawk, or something that is rustling around in the leaves on the forest floor? What do you smell? Maybe you smell rain, the dankness of the forest floor, the scent of pine, or an indescribable freshness in the air. And lastly what do you feel? Does the area make you feel happy, refreshed, peaceful, or contemplative?

Now, using your intuition, reach out to the area and see what kind of information you can pick up by sending out your thoughts to the various things around you and see if you receive a response back. You might feel strange asking intuitive questions from a mountain, but if you get a thought back that helps you move in the right direction, then say thank you. When you can feel a connection to the energy of the things that live in the natural area, whether it's a plant, an animal, or an inanimate object like a rock, then you're moving forward and progressing toward a deeper spiritual connection to the natural area you're in. If you also decide to try to obtain a more complex and even deeper level of understanding, then try visiting the same area over and over again to see what kind of new impressions you receive each time you visit. Oftentimes, you'll experience deeper connections to the energy of the place.

The energy of the natural world can help you in ways you might not expect. If you've been having problems sleeping, spending some time in nature helps soothe you at a soul level, which brings about a better night's sleep. In Norway, *friluftsliv* means "free air life" and it is a practice that says being present in nature is good for the mind, body, and spirit, which helps you on all levels including sleep (see chapter 1). If you participate in hikes or other physical activities, these will also help you sleep because you've expended your energy in the energy of nature.

One exercise I like to do when I'm in nature is to take the time to breathe in its energy. I first sense the essence of the place intuitively, then I breathe it in, allowing it to fill my entire body, not just my lungs, by imagining it flowing all through me when I inhale. I keep this energy inside me as I exhale, and then bring more in during the next inhalation. Imagining my body filled to overflowing with the energy of the natural world restores balance and positivity within me. This is an especially good exercise to do if I'm upset, angry, or frustrated. The negative emotions just vanish even though I'm not trying to send them away on an exhale. Try this exercise the next time you're in nature to see how it works for you.

Try It Now Exercise:
JUST BREATHE

Being aware of your breathing is a common way to connect to mindfulness, especially in the natural world. You can control your breathing, increase or decrease it as you desire, and when you're mindfully aware of your breathing, you're not focusing on anything else.

When I was a kid, I saw a show on television that talked about someone who could slow down their breathing until it looked like they weren't breathing at all. Well, as a kid I thought this would be a really cool thing to try to do. So I started practicing. I'd lie down on my bed and become very aware of how often I took a breath. I timed myself for a minute, counting to sixty by saying one Mississippi, two Mississippi, and so on. Then I would raise a finger every time I took a

Chapter Six

breath until I ran out of fingers then I would lower them one by one with each breath. Once I figured out how many breaths I took in a minute, then I started trying to slow down my breathing and making it shallower. In the end, I got the number of breaths down to about six in a minute. I didn't know it then, but I was using mindfulness to become aware of my breathing and to alter the way it happened. I never could accomplish my goal of looking like I wasn't breathing at all though.

For this exercise, you can try my little experiment above if you want, but I'd also like for you to do another exercise as well. Find a comfortable chair, couch, or bed or sit outside beside a tree and lean against its trunk. Now take a deep breath. Feel your lungs expand and your chest move outward. Using mindfulness, become very focused on the air coming in through your nose and leaving through your mouth. Don't push the air out, just let it flow from you. If you're outside, notice how the air and earth smells as you inhale and exhale. Now inhale deeply again. And exhale. Do this several times until you feel in sync with your breathing. On the next breath, imagine the air traveling through your entire body, not just your lungs. Consider how this feels to you. Does it make you feel tingly all over or maybe it has a calming effect on your limbs and they now feel heavier and more relaxed. Notice the sensations the inhalation has on your body but don't dwell on it. Continue breathing in and out slowly. Now I want you to give your breathing the purpose of making you relax. Feel your body getting heavier with each exhale. Keep doing this until you're completely at ease and feel peacefulness all around you. If thoughts pop into your head while you're doing this exercise, note them, but don't let your focus go to them, instead, keep your focus on your breathing, which should be slow and steady.

Now I'd like for you to give your breathing the intention of lifting you up, giving your body energy as you come back to an awakened state. Gradually increase the pace of your breathing until your inhalations are closer and closer together. By the time you're back to a fully alert stage, your breathing will be like you're panting. Mindfully increasing the pace of your breathing is very energizing and will make your awareness tingle. Open your eyes and take one long breath in and one long exhale out. Do this three times. This exercise is equivalent to taking a power nap. You'll feel energized for the rest of the day but very calm inside.

Spiritual Growth through Nature

As spiritual beings, we crave the connection to the spiritual realm, the calm, cozy feeling of complete and unconditional love that we feel when we exist in spirit. One of the ways to achieve this feeling is to find ways we can grow spiritually through nature. Spiritual growth means to become more aware of your own inner essence, to understand your own spiritual truths, to connect to your core life purpose, and to share your light with the world. When you're living within your own spirituality, then your life becomes more simplistic and cozy.

While you're searching for your spiritual truths, spending time in nature can help you attune quickly to the truth within your soul. There's just something about looking at a huge snow-capped mountain or the vastness of the ocean that puts life in perspective. You may feel small in comparison, but your energy, your core essence, is just as big and just as inspiring.

Chapter Six

When you look in a mirror can you see the universe in your eyes? It's there—you just have to connect with its energy.

When you're growing spiritually, you'll examine what you believe in and why you believe the way you do. If you spend time in nature contemplating your beliefs, the stillness of nature can help you to see your belief system clearly. Sitting quietly on a rock or tree stump and thinking about why you're on the planet while hearing the flutter of leaves in the wind can really strike a chord within you. Examine if your beliefs are aiding your spiritual growth or if they are holding you back. Do they flow as freely as the wind through the pines or do you feel blocked? Do you have ideas you're unsure about or that you're questioning?

If your beliefs are helping you grow spiritually, then you're on the right track. If they're raising questions that help you sort through your beliefs, then you're still on the right track. But if your beliefs aren't serving the purpose of helping you grow as an individual and in spirit but are instead holding you back because they're fear-based beliefs someone else has placed upon you, then now is the time to reexamine them and decide if you should let them go or change them in some way.

There is a magical quality about being outside at sunrise, at sunset, or at night with millions of stars twinkling overhead. These are excellent times to connect with your inner spirit, expand your ideals, or consider new paths to venture down, all while watching the majestic beauty of the world around you. Quite simply, being in nature helps you think. It gives your mind what it needs to settle down, to quit working overtime for just a few moments and to just be one with the world, breathing the fresh air and feeling the elements of nature all around you. Experience friluftsliv (see chapter 1) to its fullest.

As you spend time contemplating your own spirituality while in nature, take the time to really look around you and notice nature. Pay attention to the insects, plants, animals, smells, and the way you feel about all of the things you see. Each time you're in nature, look for something new and contemplate how this could be a message for you to use in your everyday life. The amount of spiritual growth you can achieve by spending time in nature is unlimited. Spend as much time as you need to reach the level of spiritual growth you'd like to achieve in life.

THE ALLURE OF BEING IN THE FOREST

Have you ever considered why the forest has such a fascination for a lot of people? Being in the woods, deep in a forest, is a mysterious power that we're drawn to. Maybe this comes from days gone by in the history of man when humans lived, hunted, and survived deep in the forest. Not everyone would choose to live in the woods; although many people do. For some, they're used to living in towns and cities because it's easier to find work so they can support themselves. Even if you live and work in the city, taking time to visit a forest can give you a new perspective, and then you may begin to feel drawn to being in nature more. Even for those who don't enjoy a stroll through the woods, if you connect spiritually and intuitively, then you can learn from the energy of the woods. I believe we're drawn to the forest because it touches us deep inside at a primal level, connecting Earth to Spirit and Spirit to Earth. It is the essence of home, of what is natural to this planet. It is the adventurer

Chapter Six

within us that seeks to discover the secrets of the woods. It is a pathway to the spiritual, to the Divine, if we'd only sit, listen, and learn from the energy that is within. This may be why the Japanese practice of shinrin-yoku, "forest bathing," (see chapter 1) is gaining in popularity.

The forest is a living thing, one of purity, simplicity, honesty, and love. How can you get all of this from plants and trees? It's more than the that—it's the spirit of the place that embraces these emotions, and when you're connected with that spirit in your own core being, then you can carry these feelings and anything you've learned from the experience back home with you. Being in the forest creates feelings of belonging to something bigger than yourself. In fact, I know that being in the forest really makes me feel small and humble when I consider myself in the grand scheme of the universe.

Some people dislike the forest because they are afraid of it. For these people, the allure of the forest isn't there, but it could be if they'd take a moment to give it a try. The forest is often depicted as a place of evil in movies. It's a place where insects, reptiles, and big animals live; there's dirt that smells weird, spiderwebs, and, well, the list could go on and on if someone was looking for an excuse not to try a walk in the woods. These types of fears can prevent people from experiencing the beauty of the forest and the spiritual connections that can be made there.

One thing I want to mention is, if you decide to take a walk in the forest, just don't grab your hat and go. Make some preparations to ensure your safety and well-being. Always let someone know where you're going and approximately how long you expect to be gone. Take your cell phone and a backup battery and turn on your GPS so you can be found easily if you get turned around. If you don't have a smartphone with GPS then learn how to read a compass and carry one with you. Make sure you also take plenty of water, a watch, and some snacks. It's easy to get turned around in the forest, and even the most avid forest-goers take these precautions to ensure that if they do get lost, they can be found easily.

Try It Now Exercise:
CREATE A PLANT SANCTUARY

In this exercise you're going to create an area either within your home, on your porch or in your yard that will be your plant sanctuary. If you are using an entire room for your personal sanctuary, you can also create a plant sanctuary in one corner of the room in addition to including plants throughout the space.

Sunrooms are another area where you can create a plant sanctuary. It's a great space for your plants because they benefit from the sun while being inside your home where they can stay warm and toasty during the winter months. During the summer months you may want to create a perennial garden in a section of your yard that has some shade. You can add a hammock, chairs, benches, or other things that you can sit on while enjoying the blooming flowers. If you also include some winter garden plants in your design, then your garden will bloom year round. Seeing beautiful blooms peeking up through the snow can lighten a dark winter mood and add to an overall feeling of coziness. Some to consider are camellia, holly, heather, winterberry, winter jasmine, firethorn, corkscrew hazel, red twig dogwood, hellebore and cyclamen.

Chapter Six

There's also the option of building a small greenhouse in your backyard.

When creating your plant sanctuary there are a few things to keep in mind. When selecting the actual plants, make sure they are ones that will all thrive in a similar environment. Consider the temperature, humidity, and amount of light inside the space. You'll also want to make sure the plants are organized in a pleasing manner. To accomplish this use plant stands, shelves, pots, and hanging planters. You may consider putting plants that grow upright in the pots, plants that are vine-like in the hanging planters and a mixture of both types of plants on the shelves. When you look around your plant sanctuary, you'll want to see a variety of plants organized in a pleasing manner. Make sure that you've left enough space around the plants. You don't want to have them crammed up against each other. They need room to grow, to spread their branches and leaves so that they can show off their beauty.

You can also get very creative with your plant sanctuary. You could use cinderblocks to create a unique display, or maybe an old wooden ladder, oversized cups for small plants or an old chest of drawers where you pull out several of the drawers and fill them with plants.

Now it's time to put it all together. If you haven't already chosen the location for your plant sanctuary, then that's the first thing on your to-do list. Once you have the location then you'll take a visit to a local nursery or garden center to select your plants, pots, hanging baskets and anything else you've decided to use to decorate the area. Or, you may pick up these things little by little at yard sales or at thrift stores. Sometimes adding items that are worn and used adds more character to

Spend Time in the Natural World

the space. When you're back at home, place the items around the space until you obtain a layout that feels cozy, homey, and charming. You'll want the plant sanctuary to contain an essence of coziness. Arrange everything until you're completely happy with the feel and look of your plant sanctuary. Enjoy it often, and year round. Whenever you need down time, hanging out with your plants can help calm and center you.

THE SPIRIT OF ANIMALS

If you're spending time in the forest and in nature, you're sure to come across animals during your explorations. Communing and communicating with animals you encounter can help you achieve a greater depth of understanding of the animal kingdom and also lead to spiritual growth.

Animals often come to us when they have a message that can help us along our spiritual path. You may have heard them referred to as totem animals, spirit animals, or animal spirit guides. I call them energy animals because I work with the animal's frequency. Being able to connect your frequency with their frequency is a step into the Divine. I go into great depth with this topic in my book *Animal Frequency*. Our connection to the animal kingdom is deep, pure, and spiritual. This is especially true when you hear, feel, or simply know what their message is and what it means in regard to your life. Energy animals often appear when you're in need of guidance but don't know where to turn. They'll deliver their messages through pictures, thoughts, words, or a feeling like the answer has been draped over you like a warm blanket. Acknowledging that animals have feelings, emotions, and messages they can

Chapter Six

share with you is a way to gain a universal understanding that all things are part of the whole.

As you're spending time in nature, pay particular attention to the animals you encounter. Notice what they're doing, how they react to your presence, and what you intuitively feel while in their presence. You might encounter a deer on a trail, see a groundhog, or spot some wild turkeys. Birds are plentiful in the forest, so notice their colors, the sound of their songs, and their movement. If they get close and stare at you, they probably have a message for you. You can also receive messages from animals that aren't around you. If you are sitting quietly in nature and suddenly imagine a beautiful moose walking along the edge of a lake, even though moose don't live where you're at and there's not a lake nearby, then give the moose your inner attention, ask if it has a message for you, and then wait for an answer.

The spirits of animals can come to you at any place and any time. They'll often come to you in dreams because it's easier for them to communicate with you when you're sleeping. When we're awake, we often put up barriers that block them. If the message is important, they will continue to appear in a variety of ways. You might see an advertisement with the animal in it, then see it on television, there may be mention of it on the radio, or you might encounter it in person. If this happens repeatedly, it's time for you to really pay attention to that animal and the message it's trying to convey.

Animals, at their core, are positive creatures that follow their instincts to stay alive. They react to situations in their environments to maintain balance in their world. We can relate to animals, and it is within this connection that we can learn great lessons that can be applied to our own lives.

As you spend time in nature, seek out the animal life. Watch them from afar, send your energy to them, and ask that they connect with you so you may learn from them. The information you receive is often extremely enlightening, is specific to your own situation, and will help you along your spiritual path.

PICK A POWER PLACE

There are many sacred sites around the world that draw people to them every year due to the intense powerful energy associated with the location. My book, *Earth Frequency*, covers in detail many of the power places and sacred sites around the world. Some of these sites have existed since ancient times and are filled with legend and reports of miraculous experiences by those who visit them. Some sites are believed to have healing powers, while others offer energy that aids in spiritual enlightenment and are inspirational. Many are surrounded in intrigue and mystery as to their origin and how the people who lived when they were created were able to accomplish such grand building achievements. These sacred sites are often referred to as power places due to the energy in the area. Stonehenge, Mount Olympus, Machu Picchu, the Pyramids at Giza, Easter Island, Chichén Itzá, and Angkor Wat are some of the most popular sacred sites, but there are thousands throughout the world, millions if you include the unknown but naturally occurring power places in nature.

While many power places are often ancient and are viewed by many people during tours or while they're on vacation, the

Chapter Six

powerful energy of the earth can be found at any place where the energy is positive and transformative. You probably have a power place close to where you live. If you've ever visited a place and suddenly feel the energy of the area change, then you're probably in a power place. In this area, the air may feel electrified, you might feel more energized, or you suddenly feel uneasy, lightheaded, or as if the ground beneath your feet is pulsing. I've often come across power places while taking walks in the woods. The energy is drawing, as if you must stand in that particular place for a moment, and when you do, you're overcome with a feeling of calm peace, of heightened awareness, and an increase in your intuition.

If you encounter a power place while in nature, take a few minutes to still your mind. Allow yourself to feel the energy of the place and notice how it is affecting you. Do you feel a chill, goosebumps, or a tingling sensation? This is an indication that you're connecting to the energy of the place. Feel the energy of the earth as it moves upward from the ground into the air. Notice how the air feels to you. Is it cooler, warmer, and more energized or does it feel calm and balanced? Pay attention to any impressions you receive while in the place. When you feel you're ready to move on, thank the earth for sharing its energy with you. As you leave a power place, you'll often feel the change in the energy of the air as you walk out of the vortex of the place's energy.

Once you've felt the energy of a power place, you'll know what to look for in the future. This is why it's often a good idea to visit a well-known power place near you just so you can feel how it is different than other places. It's an awareness you'll never forget. Once discovered, you can visit the power place anytime you need an energy boost or want to develop your own spirituality through energy work.

FREQUENCY OF SEASONS FOR SPIRITUAL GROWTH

Spring, summer, fall, and winter—what did you think of when you read each of those words? Each season is associated with specific attributes that are important for the life cycles on Earth. The four seasons each have a unique individual frequency. When I wrote those words, I thought of living in Virginia and watching how the seasons change there. In South Florida, because it's a tropical climate, you see very little seasonal changes. Sure, we might get a few cold fronts that drop the temperatures to the low 40s but it never gets any colder than that here. I miss the changing of seasons and like to return home when I can to experience them.

The seasons change because of the amount of light we receive from the sun. These changes affect us emotionally, mentally, and physically. For example, it's harder for us to absorb vitamin D in the winter, which can bring on the blues. But if you choose to connect with the frequency of the seasons, you can bring about spiritual growth for yourself. Let's take a look at each season to see how we can benefit from connecting with its frequency. While connecting to its energy during the season is more powerful, you can connect to its frequency at any other time of the year as needed too.

Spring is known as a time of rebirth. Animals are born in the spring, plants start to grow again, and the earth turns green with this new life. Flowers bloom, rainbows form after spring

Chapter Six

showers, and even the rain itself feels fresh, new, and alive. It is a time of transformation from the bleakness of winter to the brightness of spring. The frequency of spring feels like a happy laugh, a quick, playful kiss; it is overflowing with joy, bursting with energy, and it makes you want to smile and dance. Connecting with the energy of spring can help you any time you need to begin a new project, want to kick start a new health regiment, or if you need inspiration.

Summer is a time of getting things done, taking action, and living with abundant energy and positivity. The frequency of summer means that nothing is hidden in the shadows; everything has come to light. The days are longer, hotter, and filled with unlimited possibilities. This is a time to move, to enjoy life to its fullest, to sweat, to sing, to play, and to travel. The frequency of summer is joyful, fun, and exciting. It feels refreshing, as if you dove into a swimming pool on a hot day. It sizzles with possibilities and joy. The frequency of summer can help you finish projects in a timely manner, increase your productivity, and harvest and enjoy the fruits of your labor.

Fall is a time of transition, of letting go, settling, and getting ready to rest. It is a time of reflection, of contemplation, of planning, and of slowing down. Animals are getting ready to hibernate or are stocking up on food for the winter, the leaves on the trees brighten the world with their death, and a chill sneaks into the air. Connecting to the frequency of fall aids you when you're releasing something from your life to allow something new to come in, when you're planning and preparing, and when you need to stock up on supplies or get ahead in your work.

Winter is when the earth sleeps. Plants have gone dormant, the animals are hunkered down, and it's cold, icy, and snowy outside. The wind may blow cold and frigid, and it's a time to stay inside where you can turn up the heat and enjoy the coziness of hygge (see chapter 1). Winter's frequency is bold, harsh, and feels strict and strong. It can help you when you're rebuilding, or when you're out of balance and need the strength of being grounded to bring you back into balance. It is also a time of family, friends, and comfort around a fire or internally created light. It is celebration in the heart of night. It is the darkness before the light.

Try It Now Exercise:
TAKE A HIKE OR GO CAMPING

When was the last time you went for a hike or went camping? Usually you'd do these activities during the summer, but you can also enjoy a hike during the winter even if you're not camping. For this exercise, consider doing it during the summer months or choose an outdoor winter activity prevalent in your area.

It's been years since I've been camping, but I remember going like it was yesterday. The sound of the water lapping against the shore of the nearby lake, the whisper of the wind through the trees, the sound of crickets, night birds, and owls that lulled me to sleep inside of a great big red tent. Camping is a great way to get back to nature, to reconnect to your spiritual self, and to experience the joy of the forest. Whether hiking or camping, when you're around a lot of trees you'll breathe in more oxygen, which helps your overall health and makes you

Chapter Six

feel happier and less stressed. You function better with more oxygen in your system.

You can choose to go hiking or camping or to do both in the same outing if you prefer. For this exercise, let's look at it as if you're doing the two things separately. If you're going to go hiking, the first thing to decide is if you're going to go alone or if you're going to hike with a friend. If you're hiking with a friend, it's a good idea to set some ground rules so that there is a minimum amount of talking going on. That way you both can enjoy the spiritual benefits of hiking.

Next, choose the trail you plan to hike. There are many different trails to choose from that are open to the public. I highly recommend hiking public trails with a friend or two just for the safety factor. Also consider your athletic ability when you're selecting the trail. Some have a higher level of difficulty than others, so don't overdo it. Make sure you take plenty of water on your hike so you don't get dehydrated.

For a camping trip, planning is essential. You'll need to make sure that you're taking everything you're going to need with you to the campground. Granted many campgrounds offer amenities that you can purchase on-site, but if you're roughing it in the middle of the woods, you can't run down to the snack machine to grab something before turning in for the night. Make a list and check it multiple times. You might even compare your list to an official camping list online to make sure you haven't forgotten anything. You'll need to plan your meals, buy the ingredients, and make sure they're stored so they don't spoil or are in cans. Don't forget the marshmallows because toasting them over an open flame is a lot of fun. Or you can camp near a lake, go fishing during the day, and have your daily catch for dinner. There's something to be said about catching and eating your dinner like our ancestors did. It helps you get back to basics, to feel a connection to the earth and to our history as humans.

You can also choose to plan a camping trip that encompasses hiking in your daytime adventures. Remember that no two camping trips are the same. Weather plays an important part and a sunny camping trip is a lot different than one where it's raining the whole time. Still the experience is one you'll never forget.

Chapter Seven

EMOTIONAL COZINESS

Finding ways to elevate your emotional coziness is just as important, if not more so, as creating a cozy environment in which to live. There are many ways you can learn to connect with your emotions, address negativity, increase positivity, and work through any feelings that aren't helping your greater good. To get started, first look at your attitude and decide if you're in a cozy state of mind.

CHANGE YOUR ATTITUDE

Coziness is all about attitude. It's the way you think to bring warmth, love, friendship, and a feeling of well-being into your home, at work, and in the way you live. If you're not in the right frame of mind, then that warm, fuzzy feeling you're looking for and want to achieve may seem elusive at best. Changing your attitude can bring about deep transformations that can help you reach the levels of coziness you're seeking. Changing your attitude happens when you change your perspective because things are no longer working the way they once were.

Chapter Seven

Have you ever been stuck in a rut? This happens when your attitude becomes one of compliance. You're not motivated to make the changes that need to happen to get you out of the rut. Feeling stuck is the soul's way to kick-start us into action and to keep us moving forward on our life path. If you're not happy with the direction your life is taking and want to make changes, the first thing to do is to look at your attitude. The power is within you to change the way you think about things, to see situations in a different light, and to view the perspectives of all involved instead of just assuming you know what is going on.

Changing your attitude means you're letting go of negative emotions, fears, and indecision. It means you're looking at the glass as half full and not half empty. You begin to notice possibilities in everything and opportunities pop up unexpectedly because you're more aware. They were probably there all along, but it took the change in your attitude for you to see them.

When you transform spiritually, you're changing from the inside out, which affects your beliefs, actions, and the way you react to situations. It is life altering and usually lasts for the rest of your life. Changing your attitude can be so dramatic that it can be considered a spiritual transformation. You may not have realized how wonderful your life could be if you've been living with an attitude of hate, avoidance, or rebellion. Once you change your attitude to one of love, facing situations, and cooperating with others, then a whole new world opens up to you.

Examining your attitude (try making a pro/con list and be truthful) can be very eye-opening, especially if you tend to have a negative outlook on life or realized that people are telling you "don't be so negative" all of the time. Suppose you thought you were a kind person, but then you realize that you tend to snap at everyone around you. Once you recognize this, you can look at the situation to see why you're out of balance. Upon further examination, you realize you're not getting enough sleep at night, which is making you grouchy and short tempered, and you hadn't even realized it until now. You fix this by going to sleep earlier, and soon you are feeling better. It takes a truthful and careful examination of your current attitude before you can make the changes necessary to make your life more cozy, relaxed, and enjoyable.

Negativity can hold you back from thinking in a clear, positive way. It can make you feel jealousy when there's no reason to be jealous, or make you envious of what another person has. When you remove these negative emotions, then you've changed your attitude, which can alter the overall cozy factor within your life.

EMPOWER THE SELF-SABOTAGING YOU

Do you sabotage yourself? You may be doing so without even realizing it, so let's go over some self-sabotaging behaviors and how you can empower yourself instead. When you set a goal, and then do everything you can to not achieve that goal, that's self-sabotaging behavior. It's doing things to make sure you fail. Sabotaging yourself is really defeating the purpose of trying to move forward on your path. It can be frustrating because quite often the person isn't consciously trying to fail, so when they make a mistake that causes failure they come up

Chapter Seven

with excuses, when being more aware could prevent the majority of self-sabotage.

Have you ever done something before thinking it through or considering what the consequences might be? Then after the fact wonder, *why in the world did I do that*? It's fun to be impulsive and just take off for the beach for a day when you have no other responsibilities that you have to take care of, but it's self-sabotaging to lose your temper over something at work and scream at your boss when you know that type of behavior could get you fired. Thinking before taking action can prevent self-sabotaging actions.

To empower yourself, start believing in yourself. You deserve to achieve anything you want in life. Make a conscious effort to be more aware of your actions and notice when you're sabotaging your own best efforts. Once you're able to notice when you're sabotaging yourself, then it's easier to make changes when you recognize your patterns of behavior. Focus on your intentions—the reasons behind your actions. If you pick a fight with someone because you know that will push them away, examine what your real intention is—are you afraid of getting too close to someone because you think you might get hurt? If you recognize your motivations and intentions are based in negativity, then changing to a positive mind-set will help to change them. If you're not sure, write down and examine the thoughts you put on paper. Sometimes you can see motivation and intention clearer when you write it down.

As you work toward ridding yourself of self-sabotaging behavior, keep a record of the behaviors you want to change. Make notes when you experience the behavior and whether you were able to prevent yourself from falling into self-sabotage. Create a reward system for yourself so that each time you're successful you do something nice for yourself. It might take a little time but you can eliminate self-sabotaging behavior from your life.

Gratitude And Thankfulness

Gratitude, thankfulness, and appreciation are the core components of living with an intimate warm feeling of love, which is part of an overall feeling of coziness, and the basis of having a strong mind, body, and spirit connection. If we practice gratitude and seek out the sacred, then this leads to transformative experiences that allow us to become whole at the fundamental core of our beings. When you think of having an internal feeling of spiritual coziness within your life and your spirit, you think of warmth, appreciation, kindness, and all of the positive, happy emotions that go along with it. We are free in mind and spirit to express all of these emotions to those around us, which leads to happy, joyful, cozy times with others.

When we're in tune with these feelings it also makes us joyful inside. People can spend lifetimes trying to reach a feeling of wholeness, of ultimate well-being, of feeling complete. It is the search for contentment, of feeling one in mind, body and spirit, an equalization between the disconnection of the physical body and the spiritual body. If you look beyond the physical and into the spiritual realm, you'll be able to find that feeling of wholeness.

Thankfulness, especially when you're mindfully thankful, can help you obtain a feeling of wholeness. If you feel something is lacking in your life, if you've lost that cozy feeling,

Chapter Seven

or if you're waiting for someone else or a material object to make you feel cozy and complete, then you've gotten off track somehow. You're looking for something outside of yourself to make you feel whole when the only place that you can achieve it is inside yourself by seeking spiritual coziness.

There are many ways that gratitude can help you bring coziness and wholeness into your life. You can start by being present and living in the moment, in the *now*. Make the most of every opportunity instead of getting caught up in the mundane and letting special moments pass you by. You can also look at the needs of others more than your own personal needs. When you're thankful for the positives in your life, and then look outside of yourself to the needs of another, then not only does that give you a sense of gratitude for them but you can also help them achieve coziness in their lives by lending a helping hand. Giving without expecting anything in return is a gift from one soul to another. If you want to help someone else, but don't know where to start, just look around you. There are many people who are in desperate need of help in one form or another but who will refuse to ask for it. Along these same lines, if someone needs emotional support, you can be a shoulder for them to cry on—even if you don't know them. Sometimes people just need to get things out. You can also add more coziness to your life by making changes when you need them instead of putting them off due to fear. Be bold, take a step forward and throw caution to the wind. You might just find that the very thing you've been looking for is right around the next bend.

My favorite way to add coziness to my life is to smile often. I sign all of my emails with *Smiles, Melissa* and often times I'll get responses with *Smiles Back!* When you share a smile, whether in person, in an email, or through your voice on the phone, you're sharing the warmth of your inner essence, the light of your soul, and the love within you. So smile more, love more, and be grateful for every part of your life.

WORKING YOUR WAY THROUGH FRUSTRATION

It's difficult to feel cozy when frustration is around. When you're feeling frustrated, negativity is just having a field day with your energy. Everything you try to achieve fails, situations aren't going the way you want them too, and there's nothing you can do to change them. Everything that could go wrong does go wrong and things just seem to layer one on top of another until you feel like you're going to explode. When that happens, you end up taking your frustrations out on others, usually those you love. That's a horrible place to be, isn't it? When frustration sneaks up on you try to stop it in its tracks before it gets you tight within its clutches.

Everyone has experienced the irritation that goes along with frustration at some point in their lives. It's human nature. It's what you do with frustration when you feel it coming on that's important. There's no magic pill to get rid of it but you can stop it in its tracks by being aware of what's happening and taking specific steps to work through it. Frustration usually happens because you're having a bad day, but sometimes it happens when you're experiencing change and growth on a personal or spiritual level. Sometimes these lessons can be extremely frustrating until we figure out what the lesson is, then there's an *aha* moment of clarity that happens when acknowledge your frustration and realize that the emotion is

Chapter Seven

sending you a message that you need to address. Instead of letting frustration get the best of you, try looking at it as a gift you have to work through, the package you have to unwrap, to find out what is inside so that you can turn it into a positive. You can also connect to sisu, the Finnish art of courage (see chapter 1) that allows you to embrace your inner strength and courage so you can move forward through difficulties or frustration and overcome them to be successful.

We can't change the people who add to our frustration, but we can change our view of them. Instead of looking at the negative, look for the positive within the negative. If you're constantly battling against things that are out of your control then it's like paddling upstream against the current. What would happen if you simply turned around and went downstream with the water? Since you're now moving with the flow, you're no longer struggling to paddle faster than the water is pushing you. Now, you simply guide the craft with the paddles and let the water carry you along. If you view the situations that are causing you frustration, that are causing you to struggle, with this mindset, and you change your direction, then you've changed your course, eliminated the struggle and the frustration. When you let go of frustration, you're releasing negative energy and allowing yourself the freedom to step away from it. Let's take a look at a few ways you can overcome frustration.

One of my favorite ways to get rid of frustration is to do something that will allow me to disengage my mind for a little while and shift my focus and energy elsewhere. I usually head out to the barn to groom a horse or muck a stall, which allows me to settle myself and consider the situation while I'm *outside* of the situation. You might decide to clean your house, work out, sort laundry, or whittle a piece of wood to get settled and resolve why you're frustrated. If you're frustrated about a mistake you've made, stop worrying about it, own it, and move on. Time spent worrying about what you could have or should have done differently isn't going to change what happened. Lastly, think of something that is worse than what you're experiencing. It will make your frustration seem like nothing in comparison, which makes it easier to work through. Taking the time to deal with frustrations when they start can prevent you from letting it overwhelm you.

Finding Forgiveness

When you are able to forgive someone for past wrongs then you are rising above negativity to a place of understanding while letting go of negative emotions such as anger, resentment, and hatred. I'm not talking about forced forgiveness—when you say you're forgiving someone but in your heart you're really not—because that doesn't mean a thing. You're just giving lip service to the words. Forced forgiveness can cut you off from acknowledging the truth of your soul, to seeing past the immediate action and acknowledging the person and their actions on a spiritual level.

To truly forgive, and mean it, is not always easy to do. It can be really, really hard to forgive and, in some instances, another person's actions against you are unforgiveable. If you can forgive the unforgiveable, then that is a powerful leap in spiritual growth. Remember that, as spiritual beings, we all have life lessons to learn and we made agreements with other people before birth to help us learn these lessons. If they're

Chapter Seven

fulfilling their part, and we're learning the lesson, then, at a soul level, we should try to find a way to forgive them. If we don't, then this lesson will be repeated in a future lifetime until the lesson is learned and, ultimately, forgiveness given.

How do you forgive? Unfortunately, it's not as easy as speaking the words. In order to forgive, you have to understand, become aware of, and acknowledge why you're feeling hurt or wounded by another person's actions before you can let go of the negative emotions you're feeling because of them. It's up to you to make yourself feel better about the situation and heal the hurt within, to pursue your own sense of well-being, and to find your inner happiness.

I love lists, so when I feel hurt by someone else's actions, I write down what I'm feeling, why I feel hurt by what was said or done, and what I can do to change my own feelings or to clear the air. Sometimes it's as simple as telling the person that they hurt me and why I feel that way. They might not even realize that their actions were hurtful. If they don't respond in a reconciliatory manner to try to resolve the situation and start over with a clean slate, I acknowledge that fact and let it go. I know I can't change other people and if I give the situation my best effort and don't get a good response from the person in return, then there's nothing else I can do about it. If it's someone I have to continue to have in my life for whatever reasons, I find it in my heart to forgive their actions, even if I don't tell them that I've forgiven them. Afterwards, I just keep an emotional and physical distance from them because I choose not to put myself in a position where I'll be hurt again. I also do this same thing if I've messed up and need to forgive myself. I write it down, work it out, and while I can't walk away or avoid myself, I find a way to make things right within me. Forgiving yourself can be just as difficult as forgiving others.

Looking out for your own well-being is not selfish. You deserve to be treated with respect and kindness. If you're not okay with a situation, it's your prerogative to stay away from the people involved who don't have your best interests at heart. Forgiving them doesn't mean you have to resolve things with them (especially if you tried and it didn't work), nor does it mean accepting that their behavior is okay. If they hurt you, it's not okay for you. It means that you stop taking the situation personally and know that it is the other person who needs to work on their own character. Sometimes it's in your best interest to just forgive them, learn your own lesson from the experience, and move on.

You may be wondering what forgiveness has to do with living a cozy life. Consider this—if you're upset, angry, or harboring feelings of revenge or resentment, then that's on the other end of the spectrum from living in coziness. Living like this can eat away at you, making you sick and unhappy. Forgiveness means regaining the feeling of warmth and coziness within yourself by letting go of the negatives that are holding you back from the wonderful life you deserve to live.

SEEK OUT THE SACRED

One of the ways you can bring more emotional coziness into your life is to seek out the sacred. This means to look for the things that feel sacred to you, not to someone else. Sacredness is different for everyone. Seeking out the sacred helps us to broaden our horizons, alter our perception, and see the spiritual connection, through mind, body, and spirit that we

Chapter Seven

have within ourselves. It helps you attain a calm inner peacefulness, which makes it easier to analyze your emotions and bring about cozy feelings. It can be healing, calming, transformative, and add warmth and coziness to your life.

What makes your life sacred? What is deep within your soul essence that makes you extraordinary? When you connect with your own unique sacredness, it changes how you live and interact with others. Seeking out the sacred can be religious, then again it may not be. It could be spiritual wisdom, a connection to a place, being able to connect with the frequency of animals, helping those who are sick, or anything else that is important and meaningful to you on a soul level. Your connection to the Divine, the value you place on your life, and what you do with that life are all parts of the sacred. To recognize the sacred in your life, the first thing you have to do is look for it. We often ignore the things that should take importance, even when they're right in front of us. When we can become mindful and appreciative of these things, then that's a huge step in finding the sacred because you've moved past the ordinary to recognize the extraordinary. This can be transformational. Let's look at some examples. You might find it helpful to visit places that are considered sacred. There are sacred sites around the world and even in your backyard. Mountains, caves, springs, trees, rock formations, and bodies of water can have the title of a sacred site because of the earth energy that flows through the place. As a spiritual being, when you're in a spiritual place, you can connect with it. You can also find something sacred in your relationships with others, and within yourself.

Seeking out the sacred can be life altering. It transforms your perception of life and the way you think about the moments you experience. It brings about a sense of being home and of feeling that all is well within yourself and the world. The sacred helps your subconscious mind become one with your spiritual being, so you find balance, peace, and serenity. As you become connected to the sacred, clear and balanced in mind and spirit, then the body follows. You'll notice that without even purposefully trying, you start doing healthier things, get outside more, and take the time to walk and see the world around you. It's a cycle that repeats, going deeper and deeper each time as you find the sacred and let it influence you both spiritually and in your daily life.

While you're seeking the sacred, don't forget to look to the past to see where you've been, at the present to see where you are now, and toward the future to see where you're going. The lessons you've already learned will help you recognize the sacred in your life right now. It is all around you, in every fiber of your being and every part of your life, if you'll only choose to look and see it.

GENEROSITY

Generosity—helping others when they need assistance—is a key component of cozy living. When you think of being generous, you might automatically think of donating money to a cause or helping someone out financially. Generosity is so much more than that. In fact, you can be generous without spending any money at all. You can be generous with your time or emotions, or you can show generosity by acting in a kind and unselfish way toward someone.

Chapter Seven

The act of being generous is not only beneficial to the person on the receiving end of your generosity, but it's beneficial to you, too. People who are generous feel better about themselves because they were able to help someone out of the kindness of their heart without expecting anything in return. This in turn reduces the amount of stress we feel, which leads to better overall health both mentally and physically. Being generous enables us to connect to the part of our life's purpose of helping others. When we are fulfilling that life purpose, then we experience more happiness and joy. Being generous enables us to feel a richer connection to others and to feel closer and more involved with someone, therefore deepening our relationships. It boosts our confidence and can turn that internal chatterbox in our mind from negative to positive.

Being a generous person means that you also should be willing to accept the generosity of others. If you're always giving of yourself and never accepting what others want to do for you, then you're out of balance and are preventing that person from experiencing the benefits of generosity from the viewpoint of the giver. Life is all about give and take to remain in balance.

Sharing of your knowledge is a wonderful way to be generous. When you teach others the things you've learned in life or a new skill, then you're also sharing your time with them and you're offering your kindness, ultimately expanding their horizons by letting them learn from you. Sharing what you know doesn't mean you're a know-it-all, unless you come across that way, which is showing off, not being generous.

You can also donate your time or skills. If you know how to plan and organize events, then volunteer to host an event at the local community center. Maybe you're a great tennis player who could teach beginners how to play the game. If you take generosity closer to home, maybe do something nice for your siblings or parents without being asked, like doing their chores or making dinner. Give compliments to people who seem to be having a bad day—it might just turn their day around.

Think about elderly people who can't get around well, are housebound, or who live in a nursing home full time. Even if they have family come to visit, it's always nice to meet new people. If you have an hour out of your week to go visit someone just to spend some time with them and see how they're doing, that goes a long way in brightening up their day, especially if they seldom receive visitors.

It doesn't matter how you decide to be generous, it just matters that you do it. Generosity doesn't have a size limit. It can be as simple as a smile and as extravagant as you want to make it. Generosity should come from the heart and be given freely and willingly. You will make someone else feel good and you'll feel good about yourself.

Try It Now Exercise:
GIVE WHEN IT'S NOT EXPECTED

I just love surprises, don't you? When you do the unexpected, you bring joy to other people. I'm not talking about jump-out-of-your-skin scare surprises that will make someone lose their mind. I'm talking about the cozy warmth of giving or receiving something you didn't expect like a hug, going on an outing, or having takeout dinner when you're too tired to cook. When you

Chapter Seven

give when it's not expected, the person on the receiving end may feel different emotions. They may feel a sense of relief if you just did for them something that they didn't have the time to do and were worried about getting it finished, or they may feel thankfulness and joy.

Here are three examples of ways you can give when it's not expected. You can choose to do one a day or make a point to go out and do all three in one day. How you give is up to you. This exercise is to get you started.

There's a new trend going around that you can participate in that will surprise someone else with your unexpected gift. It's becoming popular to pay for the person's meal behind you in the drive-through at a fast food restaurant. I've even seen it happen in a regular restaurant and sandwich shop. I like the drive-through because the person can't argue with you or refuse to accept your gift. You've already paid and driven away, so there's nothing they can do. When this happens, there's more likelihood that they'll pay this unexpected gift forward by purchasing someone else's meal for them in the future.

Another way to give when it's unexpected is when you go to the store. Choose to park in the section that has the most people. Then, as you're walking to the store, offer to take someone's cart for them as you pass by. Usually you'll be rewarded with a big smile and thank you because you've saved them from having to walk it back to the store. While you're shopping, look for someone who may be struggling to reach something that is out of their reach but within yours and offer to get it for them. Start up a conversation with someone in line near you just to enjoy being sociable. Make your trip to the grocery store, or wherever you have to go shopping, one of being generous and kind. It'll put a smile on your face and other people's.

Have you ever missed someone that you haven't seen in a while? I have and when I get that feeling I pick up the phone and call them to just catch up and to see how they're doing. Calling unexpectedly and for no reason other than to find out how the other person is doing, and not talking all about yourself, is a way to give of yourself while reconnecting to the other person. A surprise visit is always fun too, but make sure ahead of time that the other person will be available when you plan to arrive. You don't want to drive two hours to surprise someone only to find out that they're on vacation for a week.

The more you give in unexpected ways, the more it becomes part of your everyday life. Reconnecting to your spiritual self allows you to give more of yourself to others. Doing this when it's unexpected adds the element of surprise and fun.

RELEASE RESENTMENT

Resentment is defined as feeling or showing displeasure at a person, action, or remark resulting in an injury or insult. It is an emotion that can block you from appreciating the good things in your life, it can lower your frequency, and it can cause stress to build up within you because you're so focused on hanging on to it. It fills you with feelings of ill will toward another person who you believe has wronged you. The belief could come from a situation that is real and justified, but it can also come from situations where you're imagining something that isn't there, which is often the case with jealousy.

Chapter Seven

Resentments can affect how you live right now. If there are things that happened in your past and you're still holding on to, reexamine them and decide if it's really worth holding on to the emotion, especially if it's causing you to miss out on new things you could be experiencing now. If you're holding back part of yourself from others because someone said something negative about you in the past and you're letting it affect any new relationships you might build, then you're letting your resentment over that situation tarnish what could be a shiny new experience for you. Once resentments are no longer a part of your life, you're better able to give each new person you meet a chance to connect with you without reservation.

Unfulfilled expectations are often the cause of resentment. You expect someone to do what you want them to do, to act like you want them to act, and to be something or someone that you want them to be, not who they really are. When you put this kind of pressure on someone they will usually fail, and then you end up hurt and resenting them because they weren't what you wanted them to be. If you're trying to force your ideals, desires, and expectations on someone else who doesn't share those same feelings, it's not fair to resent that person who resisted you trying to fit them into a mold. They are unique spiritual beings just like you, and it's up to you to see them as they truly are, not as you want them to be. When you're aware, thankful, and filled with a down-to-earth feeling of coziness, then resentment can't survive. It's unhealthy both physically and spiritually to hold in all of the negativity associated with resentment. At some point it will come out. You'll either get sick, stress over it too much, take it out on others, or realize that to have the cozy life that you want, you have to work through it so you can release it. If you're having a hard time letting go of resentment on your own, you might decide to seek the help of a professional who can help you see things in a different way. Instead of being miserable and wallowing in resentment, try to find a reason and a way to let it go and try snuggling up in coziness instead.

FEELING ENTITLED OR TOO PROUD

Let's take a minute to think about what life owes you. Does it owe you money, a nice house, car, boat or other material thing? Maybe it owes you love, wealth, and happiness. In actuality, *life doesn't owe you anything.* Many people will agree with this statement but there are also many people who will disagree due to a sense of entitlement. Not everyone has feelings of entitlement, but for those who do, it can make life difficult. For someone who feels entitled, who has a superiority complex, or who feels that the rules don't apply to them, they may feel that life and other people owe them something instead of understanding that you get back from life what you put into it. Someone who feels entitled believes that they deserve special privileges that others don't have or that they should be treated in special ways simply because they feel they deserve those things even though they haven't done anything to earn them. Someone who is too proud believes very similarly and is highly vested in the fact that they're never wrong in what they say, that they can do no wrong, and that you're wrong if you think they're wrong.

When you look at life from a spiritual standpoint, you'll recognize that no one is entitled to anything other than what we create and earn in this lifetime. When we're born we are

Chapter Seven

like a book that only has blank pages inside and it is up to us to fill it up with our words, our *life*. Within those words, we'll find rewards for the things we have done, the help we have offered to others, and the growth we've made on our spiritual paths. We will not find things we are entitled to just because we think they should be ours. We aren't entitled to the things we want simply because we exist nor should we feel resentment when we don't get those things. When people feel entitled, you'll often see adults having temper tantrums like a toddler when they don't get what they think they are entitled to have.

Feeling entitled or too proud can cause many problems and is a negative energy that can block your path to spiritual coziness. You could lose friends, your job, your money...you could lose it all, and then where would you be? Is that even worth it? You'd learn a difficult lesson about being more than what you really are at a soul level. Coziness can't exist when ego is running the show. If you want to create coziness in your life, if you want to transform the way you're currently living, then you have to look at what you're doing from a new perspective. When you stop feeling entitled or proud and open your heart to helping others, to considering their feelings, their wants and desires, then you are being the real you at the truth of your soul.

To eliminate a sense of entitlement or of being overly proud, try making yourself wait to get the things you want. When you have to wait for them, or meet certain goals before you allow yourself to have them, then you're creating a new respect for achievement within yourself. If you see something of yourself in what I've described, then it's a good time to do a little investigating on a soul level to evaluate how you think about things and if there's another way to achieve the things you want. By recognizing feelings of entitlement and putting a stop to those feelings you can completely transform your life.

FINDING SUCCESS IN FAILURES

Not every failure is *really* a failure. It is success in disguise. Life will sometimes throw you curve balls that puts your life out of balance when you least expect it. That's just how life is. It's what you do with these curve balls that matters. Think about how you react when something unexpected, and usually unwanted, happens. Do you get angry, upset, or frustrated? Maybe you start complaining about it or ranting over it. It's human nature to feel these emotions at the onset of the situation, but if you hang onto them and instead of working through them then they can really pull your energy down. Instead, acknowledge what happened, feel the emotions surging through you, and then try to move past them without drama. Doing this allows you to look at the situation in a clear light, through a logical and not emotional lens, and keeps you from saying things that you might regret later.

Once you have your emotions under control think about what you can do, the steps you can take to bring yourself back into balance. Some of life's curve balls can spin you completely out of control, and that too is normal, but you have to get yourself back on track to make the most of the situation and to find success in what might otherwise be considered a failure. Instead of letting it hit you and bring you to your knees, think about a baseball catcher. They'll catch a baseball and throw it where it needs to be in order to get an out or win a game. If you can grab onto the situation, turn it around and throw it back to

Chapter Seven

the Universe's pitcher, then that's a positive action based on your perspective. Seeing challenges as life lessons and opportunities to grow in spirit and on a personal basis will help you to handle any situation life throws at you.

When you feel like you've failed at something you've attempted to do, try to find the positives, the success, within the failure. Let's say you've had a bad day at work because you had so much to do that you didn't meet your productivity requirements. If you tried your best and worked as hard as you could, then let the manager know this. They don't know unless you tell them. A positive end result could be that management realizes they're asking too much of you and others in the same position, and they end up adding more people to help with the work load. All anyone can ask of you is your best and that you give 100% to what you do. If you're doing that, then you can do no more.

I'm often asked how to turn negatives into positives. It's looking for that silver lining in every situation. You can't be positive and negative at the same time, so choose to occupy your mind with the positive. Here's an example. When I first moved to Florida I was living in a temporary place and wanted to find a different apartment. I used the phone at the place I was working to call some apartments. One of the places I called charged you $50 for the call. It was well known in Florida because of the first three digits (that I don't remember now) but I had no clue. When the call showed up on the companies phone bill I was in all sorts of hot water with my employer even though I owned up to what I'd done (we weren't supposed to use the phone for personal use and this was before cell phones) and of course paid the money to them. So the negative was that I blew money I couldn't afford to blow, and got in a lot of trouble at work, and was scared to death I'd get fired over it (which I didn't) but the positive was that I learned a valuable lesson about phone numbers and I never made that mistake again. When you can learn from bad situations, work though them, and move forward from them, then you will find success in failures.

REALISTIC AND UNREALISTIC EXPECTATIONS

When you expect something, you regard it as highly likely to happen. Expectations are your feelings toward actions and events that you anticipate happening and are looking forward to. If you're living a cozy life, then you don't have overblown, unrealistic expectations of the people around you or events you want to happen. You tend to take a more even and calm approach. You will anticipate things happening, but you're not unreasonable in your actions or reactions when something doesn't happen the way you expected it to. You tend to appreciate things more when they do happen. When you have an inner sense of powerful calmness, expect the unexpected, and live with passion, then you will feel an inner peace, regardless of a situation's outcome.

Disappointments can cause you to give up any expectations you may have about things. You might think that if you don't expect anything then you'll avoid being disappointed in the future. When you think this way, you're blocking the joy you can feel in hoping and setting goals for yourself. It's fun to feel excited about possibilities instead of holding your emotions in check to avoid disappointment. If you keep your expectations realistic then you'll limit the amount of

Chapter Seven

disappointment you feel. It's when you have unrealistic expectations that disappointments can be overwhelming and feel devastating.

Creating unrealistic expectations is not only unfair to you but it's also unfair to those around you. When you expect more from someone then they can give, then you're setting yourself up to feel disappointment in their actions. Think about a situation where others expected more from you than you could give. You may feel bad because you couldn't do what they expected of you, then that amplifies when they express their disappointment in you. Instead of having unrealistic expectations of them, it's better to accept others for who they are, instead of what you want them to be. If you only expect someone to give their best and they do, then that's all that you can ask.

Putting unrealistic expectations upon yourself can cause you to feel excessive stress and out of balance. Connect with your inner essence, your true spiritual nature, then you can look past the materialistic part of life and into the Divine. Keeping your expectations real allows you to see more possibilities and opportunities than if you're stressing yourself out by pushing yourself so hard that you're wearing yourself out. You can't give your best if you're taking on too much or stressing over expectations you have of yourself that you aren't capable of achieving. When you let go of unrealistic expectations you've put upon yourself, you lighten the emotional weight you're carrying and are able to breathe and gain clarity of vision. This leads to less stress and more happiness in your life. If, instead of always pushing too hard to achieve more, you take a moment to appreciate what you've accomplished and change your expectations from unrealistic to realistic, you are experiencing soul growth. Slowing down and being realistic is part of living a cozy life.

Take a few moments to consider your expectations of yourself and others. If you keep your expectations realistic instead of unrealistic, then it is much better for your overall sense of well-being. You'll find joy instead of disappointment in situations and with other people. It is part of your spiritual nature to be in the moment, whereas having unrealistic expectations makes you miss those moments, which are so important when living in the moments of your life.

REFLECT AND PLAN

To deepen the sense of coziness within and around you, there are times when you'll need to reflect on the past and present in order to plan for the future. When you've settled into a cozy mind-set, then it's easier to look at situations in a calm, rational way, to weigh the pros and cons, and to determine the path you'll take moving forward. Reflecting helps you create a plan of action, to know all aspects of your spiritual essence better, and to see your gifts and flaws; it also allows you to change and refine what you're focused on and set new goals. We each have a divine path to follow in this lifetime to fulfill our soul's purpose and it's up to us to discover that plan and act upon it.

The weight of living in the earthly plane can push our spirituality deep within us, making it harder to discover when we're unaware. When we do connect with it, then it spills forth, letting our inner light shine for all to see. If you feel your inner light is still stuck within you, then reflecting on your spirituality can help you come up with ways you can help your

Chapter Seven

inner light break free and shine brightly. By looking where you've been, you can plan where you're going. You can make changes where you need change, find enlightenment by examining your spirituality, and create a path to more coziness, peacefulness, and happiness in your life.

To get started reflecting and raising your self-awareness to prepare for change, there are some things you'll want to think about. This is a perfect time to make a list or notes so you can review everything and make decisions later. First start with how you feel the majority of the time. Are you content, upbeat, and happy or are you unsettled, worried, and depressed? Have you been angry, jealous, or carrying around any other negative emotions that you can't seem to let go of? Are you tired or well rested? The way you're physically feeling and your emotions will affect how you're dealing with the situations in your life.

When you're reflecting, think about the actions you took in specific situations. Hindsight can often give us clarity we didn't have while we were involved in the event. As you look at your actions can you think of a way you could have gotten a better result if you'd acted differently? This is how we can determine ways to act differently in similar future situations, which will ensure an improved result. There are also times when we have to step out of our comfort zone in order to gain the results we want. If you want a more cozy life but you have a hard time letting go of drama because you crave the excitement, stress, and gossip that goes along with it, then moving away from drama will be outside of your comfort zone. You may feel uncomfortable with silence, with just being. Even if you feel a little uncomfortable, you're making forward progress.

If you make reflection and planning sessions a regular part of your life then it will help you learn more about yourself, see areas of your life that need improvement, and give you the focus and inspiration to continue to strive toward and successfully reach your goals. These sessions will leave you with a sense of purpose, of calmness, and of rationality because you are moving forward on your path.

Try It Now Exercise:
Make an Expectations List

Creating an expectations list can help you get a handle on whether you're being realistic in your expectations of yourself and others or whether you're being so unrealistic that no one, not even yourself, can meet the high levels of your expectations. If you're setting yourself up for failure because you've set the bar too high, then taking a closer look at what you're doing can be extremely helpful.

For this exercise, you can use any old notebook or loose-leaf paper. At the top of each page you're going to write an expectation. Then underneath you're going to write the following questions and give yourself space to write after each question. Be honest with yourself as you write down your answers.

1. Why do I expect this?
2. Is this expectation realistic?
3. Is this expectation unrealistic? Why?
4. Does your expectation require a period of time for adjustment?
5. How can I meet this expectation?

Chapter Seven

6. Is this expectation what really happens to me? If not, what happens instead?
7. Am I asking too much of others regarding this expectation?
8. What changes can I make to this expectation to make it easier to fulfill?
9. Am I expecting too much or am I settling for too little?
10. Am I expecting others to meet this expectation when I'm not willing to do it myself?

As you go through this list and examine each expectation you might be surprised at how you've been thinking. Many times we don't realize the expectations we've created can limit us or don't really fit with our lives. For example, if you expect everyone to do your bidding but you're not willing to do the things you're asking others to do...well, then, who left you in charge of the world as extreme emperor extraordinaire? Most people are going to balk at this kind of expectation. It's almost as if it's from the fantasy realm. If you discover that you've got expectations that are a little out of step with reality, then look at them to see why you started having this expectation in the first place.

Writing down and evaluating your expectations can give you clarity of vision. Start your examination today.

Chapter Eight

IMPROVE YOUR SPIRITUAL WELLNESS

Improving your spiritual wellness is one of the most important aspects of living a cozy life. This doesn't mean to only focus on your intuition but to expand your horizons and experience many different types of situations that will increase your spiritual wellness. Embrace all parts of your spiritual self; try new things because when the soul is ready, the teacher will come. Paying attention to your spiritual wellness will tie all parts of living a cozy life together within you.

YOGA

When you think of yoga, you might think of someone sitting on the floor with their legs crisscrossed, their hands turned palm upward on their knees and their thumb and middle finger touching, their eyes closed, while they're making an *om* sound. While this is a common position for meditation, yoga is much more than this. Yoga is a Hindu spiritual discipline. It is a way to practice meditation and relax while controlling your breathing, and it can also include going through a series of body positions called *asana*.

Chapter Eight

There are many different types of yoga but a few are more popular than others. Hatha Yoga is great for beginners because it involves gentle stretching movements that are easier to do. Hatha yoga moves include the basic moves that you'll find in more difficult disciplines. Bikram yoga is done in a studio that is heated to 105 degrees with 40 percent humidity, which replicates the environment of India. The same twenty-six movements are done repeatedly to help aid in meditation. Once you memorize the movements, they become second nature so you don't even think about them, which enables you to focus on meditation while doing the movements by rote. If you enjoy a livelier yoga session then Vinyasa yoga might be perfect for you. In this style, you move from one position to the next fairly quickly and you never repeat the same set of movements like you do in Bikram yoga. If you want to ramp up your yoga session even more, then Ashtanga yoga might be fun for you. In this style, each pose builds on the previous one with increasing difficulty.

In addition to the movements done during a yoga class, breathing is very important to both help you with the meditation part of yoga and to enable you to complete the class. *Pranayama* is the name given to the regulation of your breathing, and, like yoga, there are several different types of pranayama that you can practice depending on the style of yoga you're doing. The easiest being one called 4-4-4-4 breathing, where you breathe in as you count to four, hold your breath for four seconds, breathe out while counting to four, and holding for four seconds before breathing in again.

There are also a variety of ways to meditate while doing yoga. The Third Eye Meditation is when you focus on the area between your eyebrows where the third eye is located. Any time you feel distracted by something happening during the class or if you find yourself focusing on your movements, you redirect your thoughts back to the area of your third eye and try to silence your mind. During a Chakra Meditation, you're directed by the instructor to focus on one of your seven chakras and visualize something specific that the instructor wants you to visualize. You might also be instructed to make sounds, called mantras, during this visualization. Gazing Meditation is when you fixate your gaze on a specific item. Once you have this image clearly in your mind's eye, you close your eyes and hold the vision in your mind.

Yoga can be as simple or as complicated as you want it to be, depending on the style of yoga you choose to practice. Some styles are perfect for beginners while other styles really require you to be quite athletic to be able to keep up with the changing and holding of the different positions. The benefits of yoga for your mind, body, and spirit can be phenomenal, can bring you a sense of peace, and help you get into shape.

REIKI

Reiki (prounounced RAY-kee), by definition, is a healing technique of Japanese origin where a practitioner channels energy into the person getting the treatment in order to activate the person's natural healing ability. Reiki is thought to restore both emotional and physical wellness by clearing blockages in the body. Two Japanese words are used to create the word *Reiki*. *Rei* means "Universal Life" and *ki* means "energy." So Reiki is interpreted to mean "spiritually guided life force energy."

Chapter Eight

Mikao Usui is the person known for creating the Usui System of Natural Healing, which is his technique for working with Reiki energy and is the most popular method today. According to the Usui method, Reiki energy is passed from person to person through a line of masters with specific teachings, initiation, and form of practice. Within the Usui method, there are four different aspects of Reiki. The first is healing by laying your hands on the patient and transferring Reiki energy to them. However, many practitioners also use a hands-off method, where the hands are held a few inches above the person's body instead of touching them. The second is personal development through choices, the third is spiritual discipline though connecting with spirit and the fourth is practicing Reiki as a mystic order to connect with others following the path of Reiki. The Usui method has three symbols that are energetic keys used to access the nonphysical world. Anyone can learn the Usui method.

Reiki is the life force that flows through everything that is alive. If that energy is weak, blocked, or out of sync with the person's spirit then it can lead to an imbalance physically or emotionally. Getting a Reiki attunement is a way to bring balance to a person's energy flow, to unblock areas where the energy isn't flowing smoothly and to boost weak energy levels. Reiki is used to bring about relaxation, to facilitate healing, and to reduce stress. It is important to note that Reiki is not used to treat or cure diseases.

During a Reiki session, the practitioner uses specific hand positions to move along the person's body, seeking out areas that are holding stress or where energy is blocked and moving the Reiki energy into those areas to help heal them. The person receiving the Reiki treatment will sometimes feel a warm sensation.

If you're interested in becoming a Reiki practitioner, there are three levels of training available to you. Reiki Level 1 is also called the First Degree. It's an initiation to Reiki that teaches you to open energy channels on a physical level in order to connect with the universal life force energy. Many people who attain attunement at Level 1 use Reiki for themselves to clear their own blockages. Reiki Level 2 is also called the Second Degree, is when you learn to practice Reiki on others while also learning to expand the energy channels. During Level 2 you'll learn the Reiki symbols. You have to practice between twenty-one days and three months after your Level 1 attunement before you can receive the Level 2 attunement. Some Masters will teach both levels during an intensive weekend class and attune you to both at the same time. Reiki Level 3 is also known as the Third Degree and Reiki Master. This is the level of being a teacher who can attune others to the different levels of Reiki. It is a deep commitment to Reiki and training others in Reiki.

DANCE

Dancing is a great way to get exercise and connect with your inner essence through the sound of the music, the flow of your body, and the energy that dance creates around and within you. It gives you a sense of well-being while you're having fun. Dance helps you attain a happy, energized feeling that can transfer to other areas of your life. After dancing, your body and mind are invigorated.

Chapter Eight

Dance has many different types of benefits. Physically it requires you to move your body and use your muscles, and it helps you gain better coordination. When you're dancing regularly, the exercise will improve your muscle tone and can even help you lose weight. It is heart healthy because it is an aerobic activity, which also increases your lung capability, makes you more flexible, and gives you greater endurance. If you haven't danced for a while, you might be winded at first, unable to dance for long periods of time, and sore afterward, but keep at it to reap the long-term benefits. Mentally it also helps with your memory, especially if you're doing a style of dance that has many individualized steps like country line dancing, ballet, or tap dancing. The more you dance, the better you'll feel about yourself because it boosts your self-confidence psychologically and in your physical body.

If you're dancing with a partner, you'll have a greater awareness of the space around you and how far you can move without crashing into other dancers. If you're dancing alone, you can still attain special awareness because you have to know where you're going in your dance. Dance also improves your overall coordination and balance.

You can dance anywhere. When I have to clean my house, I crank up the music and dance around while I'm cleaning. It's more of a workout, but it makes the dull task of cleaning much more fun and entertaining. You can also join a dance school and go to classes, join competitions, or join a belly-dancing class at your local gym. Once I even did a twenty-four-hour dance marathon, and let me tell you—that was definitely a challenge. But it raised money for a great cause and was a lot of fun, even though I was exhausted when it was over. There are plenty of places to dance, you just have to seek out those that offer the style of dance you want to participate in, or you can rock out in your home if you prefer dancing in private.

When it comes to dance, age doesn't matter. Everyone loves to put a little wiggle in their hips or shimmy in their shoulders with they hear a song that they enjoy. Car dancing is also popular and I do that all of the time. I can't help but smile when I see other people driving along, sitting in their seat and moving their shoulders and head to an obvious beat. Just be safe when car dancing—no head-banging allowed because you can't see where you're going!

So turn on the music and get your body moving. You'll feel better overall, you'll smile more, and you'll feel physically refreshed for your effort. Dance as slowly or as fast as you like for your current physical condition. Try not to overdo it when you start so that you're not too sore and then give up on it. Dancing is fun and it's good for the soul.

TRAVEL

You might be wondering how traveling can help you live a cozy lifestyle. The experience of seeing the world, whether it's near or far from where you live, provides you with insights that you wouldn't have obtained by staying at home. While on your travels you will experience cozy cultures from around the world that you can include in your own life when you return home.

Traveling doesn't have to be difficult or expensive. If you can't afford to travel around the world, then find weekend travel destinations that are relatively close to where you live. Choose destinations that offer something completely different

Chapter Eight

than what you experience every day. Pick locations that can help you learn about other cultures, history, or unique local businesses. By choosing a destination outside of what you know, you're expanding your horizons and are becoming a more knowledgeable and well-adjusted person because you're learning about the world around you. Choosing to travel locally also gives you the added benefit of meeting more people who live in your area and supporting the community while having an exceptional individual travel experience.

Not only is traveling an adventure, it has many other benefits as well. You can choose to book active travel time where you'll be participating in various activities such as hiking, water sports, horseback riding, or white-water rafting. You could also choose to book a cultural tour where you are immersed in the local culture in a different country. Both of these types of travel have perks. If you're doing active traveling then you might discover that you're great at water-skiing and just didn't know it because you hadn't tried it before. Or you might get over your fear of heights long enough to cross a swinging bridge high over a river—for someone who is afraid of heights this is a major accomplishment. If you're traveling to experience local culture, then you will learn words in another language and understand how people in other countries live, which gives you a completely new perspective. Both types of travel help you to meet challenges head on, grab opportunities that come your way during your travels, and offer you the chance to learn something new about yourself along the way.

When you make the time to travel, it helps you get out of the same daily grind that you may often find yourself in. It gives you the opportunity to experience more of life instead of being stuck in a rut. Traveling will give you pleasure, new knowledge, and interactions with people you would never have met otherwise. You never know—a person you meet on your travels might become your next best friend. It also gives you great stories to tell your family and friends when you get home.

If you'd like to travel but aren't sure where to start, the first thing you'll need to do is calculate the cost of the trip that you'd like to take. There are all kinds of ways to save money along the way. Travel agents often offer all inclusive deals that can save you money on flights, hotels, and rental cars. Taking the time to travel will give you experiences that you'll treasure for your entire life. Make sure to take your camera (or smart phone) so you can capture those moments!

Focused Meditation

There are many different ways to meditate by following the traditional methods, some of which are the Buddhist, Hindu, and Chinese meditation techniques. Each of these methods has their own postures and breathing techniques. Traditional methods of meditation often require that you learn from a teacher. If you have the time to take classes in the traditional methods, then any one of them may be perfect for you.

Within the traditional methods there are three different focusing concepts you can try during meditation. You can focus on one object, on everything around you, or on nothing at all, instead focusing within. The purpose of focusing on something outside of yourself in the beginning is to train the mind to quiet down and become filled with calm peacefulness. Meditation is a way to find happiness within yourself by freeing your mind of worry, chatter, regrets, and any other emotion that brings

Chapter Eight

about inner distress. You can't be happy if your mind is in a state of distress, you can't live a cozy life if you're constantly worrying about something, and you can't be true to your own inner self if you're not at peace within your spiritual essence. Meditation can help you resolve things that are holding you back from being happy.

Meditation connects the spiritual realm with the physical realm and it's done within your soul essence. It helps you to remain in control of your inner world through feelings of calm peacefulness and spiritual coziness when things aren't going as planned. When the world around you seems to be topsy turvy, meditation can help you remain calm and at peace in difficult situations because it enables you to connect with your true spiritual essence, to see the world as a place to learn while knowing that there is more than what we see.

If you're a very busy person, you might feel you don't have the time to learn a traditional method of meditation. Or you might feel that the traditional methods are too hard, time consuming, or they might make you feel a bit overwhelmed. That doesn't mean you can't meditate though. Guided meditations are easy to do and are freely available online. You can also create your own guided meditation that hits on the things you want to work on in your life to create more positivity and happiness.

I've created my own style of meditation over the years. I'm always super busy with something or other and for me that's normal. I don't have time to practice the traditional methods, so let me share my one minute white light meditation with you. I do this meditation whenever I'm feeling out of sorts, am worried about a problem, am overwhelmed or just need a moment to refresh myself at a core level. Here's what I do. Regardless of where I am (with the exception of driving—don't do this when you're driving!) I stop what I'm doing, close my eyes, and imagine white light gathering like a cloud around the top of my head. I address the issue, say *fix it please* to the spiritual realm and then imagine the cloud of white light pouring through me like a lightning strike. It fills me quickly and fixes the issue before coming back up through me and exiting through the top of my head back into the spiritual realm. It takes away worry, feelings of being overwhelmed, and basically anything that's bothering me so I feel balanced and happy again. All of this in a minute or less. Now, I've been doing this exercise for many years so it might take you a little longer than a minute but you're welcome to try to see if it helps you too.

Try It Now Exercise:
GUIDED WELLNESS MEDITATION

For this exercise, I'm going to lead you through a guided meditation for wellness. You can also read this slowly and record it so you can play it back while you're actually doing the exercise.

(Start recording here) To begin, find a place where you can either sit comfortably in a chair or lie down on the floor or a bed. Once you're settled, imagine a wave of energy entering your body at the top of your head, slowing moving through you until it goes out through the bottom of your feet and the tips of your fingers. As this wave of energy flows through you, it makes every cell in your body relax into a heavier state. It moves very slowly, touching every cell with its relaxing effect.

Chapter Eight

Let your breathing follow the movement of the energy. Breathe in through your nose and out through your mouth. Continue this for a few minutes until you sense the energy leaving your body because you are completely relaxed.

Now focus on the following words as you listen to them being played back for you. Let your energy connect to the energy of the words; let them empower you, enhancing your overall well-being.

"I am living my life to the fullest. I am doing what is best for myself in every aspect of my life. I am aware and living in the moments of my life. I understand that I have complete control over my own energy, my frequency, and that I can allow it to raise or lower as needed. I create my life as I choose to live it. I choose to live in a cozy positive environment with people who will enhance, nurture, and improve my life. I choose to embrace the wellness within the universal flow and allow its positive effect to enhance my life in every way. I feel the energy of universal wellness wrapping around me like a blanket, holding me in a warm, cozy embrace. This is a natural process, one that I may have forgotten, but now have chosen to remember. I am one with all that is, all that was, and all that will be. I am power. I am love. I am spirit eternal. I embrace my spiritual essence and vow to live in truth to my inner being while on the earthly plane of existence. My desires manifest in the earthly plane, allowing me to achieve the goals I desire. I will make it a habit to quiet my mind every day, to relax, to think only as much as is needed to reach a resolution, and to share the love in my heart with anyone who needs it. I understand that my experiences will lead me to the place I am supposed to be on my spiritual path. I make my choices freely and without doubt. I work to raise my frequency to higher levels so I can happily enjoy the cozy lifestyle I have selected for myself. I embrace the simple, I honor the little things, and I am part of it all. My general wellness will enhance my daily happiness as I do the things I love with the people I love and for the reasons I love. I am pure, I am the light, I am love."

Imagine another wave of energy entering your body through the top of your head but this time as it moves through you it invigorates you, awakens you, mind, body, and spirit. You feel positivity in all areas of your life, an overall wellness that empowers you throughout the week. *(stop recording)*

EXPRESS YOURSELF

You are a unique person with thoughts that are different from anyone else on the planet. You see the world through your own spirit, through your own energy, and through eyes that are different than everyone else. So, how do you express yourself and your feelings while living a cozy lifestyle?

There are literally thousands of ways that you can express yourself and each one of us does it in a different way. Let's go over some of the basic ways you can express yourself, which will also keep you living in coziness. Then you can take these ideas, expound upon them, and put your own unique twist on the way you express the inner you to the world.

The primary way people express themselves is through speech. If you enjoy something you can tell someone about it, teach a class on it, or do an Internet video about it. Maybe you know how to do something that can help others learn how to do the same thing, or maybe you've created a new way to organize your home that you can share through the spoken

Chapter Eight

word. You may give excellent advice that people seek. If you prefer writing over talking then you can express yourself through your website, blog, or by writing articles for other websites. You may even be able to write a book to express your ideas. Speech and the written word are wonderful ways to express your inner thoughts, the way you do things, and to help others understand the topics you're writing or speaking about. Your facial expressions and movements when you're speaking also add another layer to the way you express yourself. You may talk with your hands or eyes in addition to normal speech. If you want to express your feelings privately, then a journal might be the way to go.

Expressing yourself through fashion and the way you present yourself to the public is also unique to you. Some people prefer to wear classic clothes and accessories that make a fashion statement while others enjoy being flamboyant in their appearance. You may like a traditional hairstyle or a new, unconventional, trendy style to express your inner self. Makeup can create a subtle or bold statement about yourself. We all have our own quirks, preferences, and styles that are all our own. In college, I had a purple rat tail that was hidden under my hair until I braided it and pulled it over my shoulder so it could be seen. Today, mermaid hair, which is a multitude of colors, is all the rage. The cologne or perfume you choose to wear adds to your fashion statements. It can be fresh and understated or bold and loud in its scent.

You can express yourself through your home decor, the way you've decorated your home to make if cozy and warm, or you might like the stark and formal look for your interior space. Whatever style you chose, it will reflect part of your inner self.

Drawing, painting, photography, creating videos, dancing, the type of music genres you enjoy—all of these are ways to express your inner self. Maybe you love cooking, baking, and inventing recipes. If so, you could host a dinner party for family or friends to show off your creations.

Regardless of the ways in which you chose to express yourself, your personality and inner light will shine through every single time. You may bring a smile to someone else's face but the fact is, through self-expression, you're making yourself happy.

VOLUNTEER

Have you ever taken the time to volunteer somewhere? Volunteering is a wonderful way to obtain a cozy feeling inside. It brings joy to be able to help others by giving of your time, energy, and soul essence. You can choose any type of volunteering. It may be as simple as jumping in to help your neighbor with some yard work, helping kids with their homework in an after-school program, helping out during times of natural disasters, or lending a hand at a local animal rescue. Volunteering helps you feel spiritually connected to the people in your community and part of something bigger than just yourself, which is very healthy for your spiritual growth. It's a positive sharing of yourself with those who can benefit from your assistance.

Have you ever heard the saying *many hands make light work*? This is what it means to be a volunteer. When more people jump in and help, the goal is accomplished in much less

Chapter Eight

time than if one person tried to do it all on their own. It is seeing a need and participating in the solution to bring relief, joy, and a sense of accomplishment to others and yourself.

When you volunteer you not only make a difference in the life of someone else, or an animal's life, but you make a difference in your own life.

Let's say you love animals but you've never had an animal. If you volunteer at an animal shelter you'll learn new skills through your experiences. Doing something you've never done before is a way to challenge yourself to achieve your goals. You may even discover that you're exceptionally good at what you volunteered to do, which helps you outside of the volunteer environment. You may even adopt one of the animals from the shelter once you're more confident in your ability to care for an animal. Volunteering is always a way to meet new people who have the same interests as you.

There are many opportunities to volunteer if you look for them. The best way to decide where you'd like to volunteer is to think about the things you like to do. There are many organizations in every field that are nonprofit and have many positions available for those who want to help. You might work in a garden, cook, teach a sport or class, do computer work, build something or help with cleanup. There are also ways to volunteer that aren't connected with a structured volunteer program. Maybe you love going to the beach and a local group is doing a beach cleanup on Saturday. It's a great way to help out while being in an environment you enjoy. Or maybe you love horses but can't have your own. Volunteering at a local barn or rescue will give you time with horses and will help those running the facility. If you enjoy spending time with the elderly, you can volunteer at a nursing home. Hospitals, libraries, and community centers usually have some type of volunteer opportunities in which you can participate.

The opportunities to volunteer and make a difference are endless. You just have to choose something that is important to you or that you enjoy doing and get involved. The rewards to volunteering are gratifying both personally, spiritually, and, if you're doing manual labor, physically. So what are you waiting for? Get out there and make a difference in someone's life today.

APPRECIATE THE ARTS

When you think of art, what comes to mind? Paintings or drawings are what most people think of first. There is much more to the arts than just painting though. If you look at any college degree program you will probably find classes in applied arts, liberal arts, fine arts, decorative arts, performing arts, and visual arts. These can be further broken down into the areas of painting, dance, ballet, music, drama, film, theater, creative writing, digital design, poetry, interior decorating, sculpture, and more. The arts can be defined as any outlet that allows you to use your creativity and imagination to create something others can enjoy and appreciate.

If you're someone who enjoys history, science, or are mechanically minded, then you may say the arts aren't for you. That's okay. You can apply what we're discussing to those fields as well. Being creative is part of feeling cozy. When you can make something, whether it is a beautiful song on the piano or a unique, intricate machine that is intriguing to watch, that creation is a part of you, of your creative soul, and when it

Chapter Eight

is shared and appreciated by others; that's the same principle as appreciating the arts.

Making another person feel a connection to your work, to move them emotionally and at a soul level, is what the arts are all about. It is taking someone away from the day-to-day routine so they can experience something extraordinary. It is an artistic endeavor that makes you think and feel from your core essence. It can raise your frequency and empower your spirit. The arts teach you to look at situations from a new perspective, to connect with your senses and to dig deeply into the well of your spiritual emotions to find a Divine connection to the experience.

You can participate in the arts as an observer or as the artist. As an observer, you can appreciate the arts by going to a theatrical production, taking a trip to a museum, supporting groups that create the arts, or visiting the screening of a new film or indie project. As an artist, you could participate in a painting class, take a dance class, or learn to play a musical instrument. Participating in, instead of just viewing, the arts allows you to stimulate your soul's creative essence and to tap into your unique talents, whatever they may be. Sharing your final creation, whether it's a performance, a painting, or a sculpture, exposes others to the arts. As an artist, you use your innate talents to let your spiritual essence shine through, which brings joy to others.

As spirit, we have always been entities of expression. Throughout time on Earth, we've always been able to find ways to bring the energy, colors, and sounds from the spiritual realm into the physical realm. Creative expression of our spiritual selves has always been a part of our being. When we're connected to this creativity, we're also connected to the energy of coziness within. Creative expression allows us to reconnect to a part of our spiritual immortality through engaging in a way to bring our creative spiritual self to life through our art.

If you haven't experienced the arts lately, take some time to experience the range of emotions you'll feel when viewing the ballet or a play, or by creating a painting that was born of your spiritual being. Let the arts inspire you to express the truth of your inner self, your true Divine essence.

Try It Now Exercise:
OVERALL WELLNESS CHECKLIST

When you think of wellness, you probably break it down into several different categories. There's physical, mental, emotional, spiritual, social, and habitual wellness. We'll go through each of these in a minute but for right now, I'd like for you to make a chart that will be your checklist for this exercise. Once you make this chart, you can use it every day, every week, for every year if you'd like. Or you can use it short term until you get back on track making your overall wellness your number one priority. At the top of the chart write Daily Wellness. Then make three columns. In the first one write Physical at the top, in the second one write Mental, in the third, Emotional, in the fourth, Spiritual, in the fifth Social and in the sixth write Habits. Under each section write something that you want to do to maintain your daily wellness.

Let's start with some examples of what you'd put under the Physical category. Draw little lines in front of each section so you can place a check mark in it when you've completed it for the day. You might write __ Walk, __Stretching, __Maintain

Chapter Eight

Straight Posture, __Jog, __Swim, __Biking, __Sit-ups, __ Weight Training, __ Push-ups, __Pull-ups, __Leg Curls and so on. You may also include your nutritional plans under physical too. Some of these might include eating salads, adding vegetables, limiting red meat, or any other thing that you're doing in regards to your menu that is beneficial to your health. You may not check off every item every day. The goal is to make sure you're improving your overall wellness. So if you have two different kinds of exercise on your list but you only did one of them; that's okay. You can do the other one tomorrow.

The section for mental wellness would include things you do to increase your intellect, to stimulate your thoughts, imagination, and motivation. Include achievements you've made at school, in your career, or in any area of your life. Think of the things that affect you mentally, that have positive or negative influences on your mind. You can put ideas here that will help you be more productive and that help you meet your true potential.

The section for emotional wellness would include things you'd do for downtime or to relieve stress. Ways you deal with highly charged emotional situations, ways to avoid or deal with depression and sadness. In this section put a list of emotions that you'd like to experience and then try to put yourself in a situation where you can. For example, if you want to experience exhilaration, ride a roller coaster. Pick something from this list each day.

The section for spiritual wellness is where you'll include things about your intuition, identifying your soul's purpose, conversations with your higher self, achieving spiritual coziness, and a list of goals you'd like to meet in regards to your spiritual growth.

The section for social wellness would include things you'd do for fun, the people you'd like to see or hang out with and events that you'd like to attend. Make sure to include both family and friends in this section.

The section for habitual wellness is where you'll list the habits you currently have that you like, or ones that you want to change or eliminate. You can also include new habits that you'd like to develop.

By completing this chart you will be able to see areas of your life where you can make changes or where you've met goals. Areas that need improvements or where negativity is outweighing positivity will be very clear when you see it in writing. You can change this chart around as needed while you're working on your spiritual growth. You can also make a more detailed chart by making one page for each of the main categories.

Chapter Nine

THE TRANSFORMATIONAL ENERGY OF SPIRITUAL COZINESS

When you connect with the spirituality of coziness, and implement it in within your spiritual self and in your daily routine, you can experience transformation in all areas of your life. Transforming yourself, your energy and the way you live will bring feelings of calm peacefulness, coziness, and joy. It will reduce stress and help you get into a state of balance. When you're balanced, your energy flows in a positive way, allowing you to be all that you want to be. Spiritual coziness can transform you in ways you may not have even imagined.

THE FREQUENCY OF LETTING GO

When you think about transforming your life, one of the first things that comes to mind is letting go of something that is holding you back, causing you stress, or that you no longer need in your life. The frequency of letting go means you're releasing a person, situation, or emotion's energy that is attached to you. If the thing you want to release didn't cause you negative feelings, then you couldn't want to let go of it. The

Chapter Nine

frequency of letting go always reminds me of an ocean wave. It swells, crashes, pulls back and swells again until finally the waters calm and the waves barely move against the shore. When you're releasing something in your life, you go through similar stages. First your emotions swell because of the situation. They may be running high, you may be upset, overly emotional or you're just feeling miserable because of someone else's actions or a situation you're in. Then you crash. You might have a melt-down, get into an argument, blow up in anger, or just give up. But then something happens and you'll feel pulled back into the situation, or reconnect with the person, and your emotions even out and you feel like everything is going to be okay now. Until something else happens that causes your emotions to swell again, just like that ocean wave until you crash onto shore. This rolling wave of the frequency of letting go will happen over and over again until you finally resolve it within yourself and decide that you no longer want to deal with the situation or person, and feeling all of those high and low emotions. It is that point, when you say I've had enough, and you release yourself from the situation, that the frequency of letting go calms and settles into the spiritual coziness of acceptance.

Energy fluctuates, that's why you can raise your frequency and why things that happen to you in life can lower it. If you can stay on an uphill momentum though, then over the long term you can keep your frequency at higher levels. Since the frequency of letting go has a definite pattern of rising and falling before it settles down into a particular even level, if you notice this while it's happening, then you can make your adjustments while on an upward swell, which can sometimes prevent the crash. Your participation level determines how hard the crash will be. For instance, if you sense that a disagreement with someone is going to get heated and turn into a full-blown argument, then you can choose to step away from the situation before it goes that far. If you do this, then the fallout from the argument (the crash of the ocean waves) will be less because you chose not to participate any longer. However, if you choose to actively engage yourself in the argument until you lose your mind and are screaming and yelling, then that crash is going to be pretty traumatic and upsetting for you.

Letting go can be difficult depending on the situation and your feelings about it. If you're not tuned into the energy surrounding it, especially the energy connected to your emotions concerning it, then it can be harder still. When a situation is exceptionally painful for you emotionally, you'll benefit from trying to put some space between the situation and yourself so that you can consider all sides without being tangled up emotionally. Every emotion you feel is valid because it belongs to you and it is how *you feel inside*. Emotions are yours to work though and connecting to the frequency of letting go can help you see the patterns, both positive and negative, in your life so that you can release what no longer serves you with ease. You'll achieve peace of mind and will embark on a new adventure in your life when you leave things you no longer need or want behind.

SUBTLE ENERGY SHIFTS

Shifts in energy can help you recognize when it's time to let something go in order to experience growth on a personal or

Chapter Nine

spiritual level. When you're going through a spiritual transformation you'll often experiences subtle signs that indicate that your frequency is elevating, that you're in tune with your core spiritual essence, and that you're connecting with the Divine. People who are going through a spiritual transformation will also notice subtle energy shifts that take physical form like random moments of forgetfulness, feeling vibrations or momentarily hear ringing in your ears, thinking you hear or see something that is manifesting from the spiritual plane, or having thoughts that are connected to the Divine.

If you're experiencing subtle energy shifts in a relationship (romantic or platonic) that's not going well, you may feel like there is distance between the two of you, as if you're not open with each other as you once were, or that you're a convenience that the other person could do without. You may also feel that your main cause of stress these days is your partner. Maybe the other person is always negative, complaining about one thing or the other, or always putting the blame on you. In cases like this you might even feel happier being alone than with your partner. These subtle shifts in energy kind of gradually creep up on you but once you notice them, they can clue you in that maybe it's time to let this relationship go. This is something you do for yourself, not for the other person. On the other hand, if you're in a relationship that is growing or developing deeper connections between the two of you, then you may feel a growing closeness, wanting to be with the other person all of the time because you enjoy their company. You may find that you're completing each other's sentences, having the same ideas, and you can communicate with just a look.

These positive energy shifts let you know that this is a relationship worth pursuing.

When you're experiencing an energy shift in your own spirituality or in a relationship, it is a sign that you're experiencing growth. Sometimes you have to let go to grow and other times, like in the case of a budding or growing relationship, you have to wait to see how it develops. During the development stage you may find that you're letting go of things in your past that are no longer serving you in order to allow the new relationship to grow.

If you can pay particular attention to the subtle energy shifts in your life as they happen, then you'll find that you'll not only be able to connect with others, to develop a feeling of security within your life, to feel more coziness, but you can also see when it's a better idea to just let go instead of trying to hang onto something that is no longer working for you.

COMMUNICATION REMEDIES

One of the ways that you can transform you life through the spirituality of coziness is to learn how to effectively communicate with the people around you. When you're on the same page and have an easy flow of communication, then life is comfortable, loving, and you feel at ease. If the ability to communicate gets jammed up and you're having problems getting your point across, the problem could be with you or it could be with the person with whom you're trying to have a discussion. Either way, the lines of communication must be cleared to get back on an even keel.

Let's take a look at some of the things you can do to remedy ineffective communication. Make sure that you're not

Chapter Nine

doing all of the talking and hogging up the conversation. It's important to listen to what other people have to say. Listening to them, and I mean *really* listening to them, and comprehending what they're saying or being empathetic to their current dilemma enables you to help create a feeling of coziness between the two of you. There's nothing worse than being in a conversation where you feel you aren't listened too. If you're on the phone you may hear the other person working on their computer and there's a pause when you ask them a question because they're not really listening to you. Or the other person may ignore your comments to keep talking about themselves. Sometimes we're not listening to the other person or they're not listening to us because of the fear of not being heard or because they really don't want to be having the conversation right now due to other things they need to do. Making sure you're listening as much as you're talking and having a balanced conversation is the best kind of conversation to have. When a friend is going through something that is difficult then you'll expect the conversation to be one sided, but just know that the next time you talk with that person the conversation may be all on your side instead of theirs.

Asking questions is important to good communication skills. You can learn information that you need or that clarifies what the other person is saying. You can also ask the other person for input on what you're talking about. This will give you a different point of view and can often give you options that you haven't considered yet. Asking questions and getting input from the person you are talking with also creates a more balanced, and comfortable, conversation where both parties feel heard and appreciated.

Depending upon the type of conversation you're having you will deliver your part in specific ways. For instance, if you're an employer talking to an employee or vice versa you'll probably be confident in tone and use concise words. You probably aren't going to get into a long story about something that happened to you just to make a point when talking to your boss, but that would be a good tactic to use if you're speaking with someone who is trying to resolve an issue and you've had a similar experience. If you come across too strong when it's not necessary, you could put the other person on the defensive without meaning to, but if you come across as too quiet you could project the image of weakness, which wouldn't be a good idea in a business meeting. Knowing the type of conversation you're having and the goals you're trying to reach will help you keep the tone balanced and the conversation comfortable and in forward motion.

Look for New Fun

Sometimes one of the quickest routes to transformation is doing something completely new to you. The activities that you do for fun can add more coziness to your life. If you're not doing enough things for your own personal enjoyment then you can get caught up in having too much to do, which can lead to stress, irritability and problems sleeping. In order to achieve the most benefits from your activities, try to change them up instead of doing the same things over and over again. If you like doing something, keep on doing it, just add more activities to those you're already doing and put them all in rotation. This way you're still doing the things you love but are trying new experiences as well. This adds variety and you never know when a new experience will be something that you love doing.

If it's hard for you to find time to do fun things, then pencil them into your schedule so that you force yourself to do something that relaxes you and makes you smile. That way you'll make sure you're getting in something fun during your workday. At times it's a good idea to take a break from work to give your mind a chance to rest and your soul a chance to soar. This is what living a cozy life is all about. Finding balance between what you *have to do* and what you *want to do*. We all are responsible for ourselves and our own personal well-being so we have to work in order to earn money to support ourselves. If we spend too much time on work and not enough time enjoying the simple things in life, like taking a moment to listen to the sound of a bird singing a song or to really feel the wind against your face, then your spiritual self suffers. Relaxing, enjoying the world we live in, and taking time to do the things we love is to our spiritual essence the same as water is to a dying plant, it is rejuvenating, invigorating, and extends life.

There is a direct correlation between how we feel inside and our external experience so it only makes sense to keep both our inner feelings and our external activities upbeat, positive, and ever changing. If you're not sure how you can add new fun, interesting, and engaging activities to your life so that you're keeping both the internal and external experiences balanced, let me give you a few ideas. When was the last time you learned how to do something new? If it's been a while, it's a good time to try something that you've always been interested in but have never accomplished. Maybe you'd like to try skydiving, or windsurfing, or deep-sea diving. Maybe you'd like to learn to paint, or sculpt, or skateboard. Anything that you find interesting, and that you don't know how to do, is fair game.

There are also lots of groups you could join so you meet others with similar interests. In fact, you can probably find a group for just about anything. Joining a group will enable you to make new friends while participating in the activity, which often leads to those same friends becoming part of your life outside of the activity.

What is fun for one person may not be fun for another. For example, someone who works as a groom in a stable might consider grooming a horse a chore that is part of their job. They do it because they have too. Or for someone who doesn't like horses, it might be as much fun as getting a tooth pulled. But for me, grooming my horses is fun and something that I enjoy. It gives me time to power down my brain, to relax, and spend time connecting with my animals. Yes, it's physical work, but there's so much more to it than that for me. Just the smell of the animal, the way it feels under my hands, the personality and energy that radiates from them as I brush them, that's relaxing for me.

As you're transforming yourself, making your life cozy and complete, look for new ways to bring fun and enjoyment into your life. Step out of your comfort zone and you might just surprise yourself.

POWER UP YOUR SPIRIT

Your spiritual being is made of energy that has a frequency all its own. When you connect to the core part of your being

Chapter Nine

where your spirit resides, you can tap into your true potential, the power of the Universe that is part of your spiritual self.

Powering up your spirit means to remember who you are at a soul level, to connect your physical mind to your spiritual self, and to remember the loving, grateful, kind, and pure being that is you. One the spiritual plane, negativity doesn't exist. It is the negativity of the earthly plane that can prevent you from remembering the spiritual plane. Once you learn to accept life as it is and understand that there is more to the human experience than what we can see with our eyes, then you're well on your way to connecting with you core spiritual essence and transforming yourself.

You'll discover that your beliefs are different and unique to you because of your experiences. For example, the majority of people may believe in a gut feeling or a mother's intuition but if you label those same feelings with the word *psychic* then there's often an immediate assumption that what that person is experiencing can be disregarded because psychics are only out to steal people's money. Unfortunately, there are some people like that in the world and it's why the term has a negative connotation but if you experience a psychic event firsthand through your own intuition, then your opinion changes. Each of us has to trust that our experiences in this lifetime are based on lessons we decided to learn while on the earthly plane. Each of these experiences brings about soul growth because we are tapping into our spiritual power.

If you'd like to take steps to purposefully power up your spirit there are several things you can do to get in touch with the light within you. Meditating will help you get in touch with your spiritual self and feel the coziness within your true self.

Some people enjoy sitting quietly for a long period of time and connecting with their inner selves for guidance, to feel the powerful energy within themselves, and to work on enhancing their connection to their spirit. Others, like myself, don't have time for long meditations, and prefer a short five minute session where you quickly feel your spiritual essence and the calm, controlled power of your inner light. Whether you choose a long or short meditation, it is a great way to connect with your spiritual power.

Gratitude also goes a long way in adding power to your spirituality. When you're thankful for the events, people, and situations in your life, even if they're not all positive, then you are expressing your spiritual power. The easy way out is to complain about the things you're experiencing that may not be in accordance with what you want in life, but it takes a special ability to access your inner power to find the silver linings, make something positive out of a negative, and to grow from your experience through thankfulness.

Being open to possibilities is another way to transform through spiritual coziness and power up your spiritual energy. In life we are often presented with situations where we can grow in spirit though being kind, going above and beyond what is expected of us, and helping others in need. When we are powered up in spirit it is easier for us to recognize and take advantage of these opportunities for soul growth. As you learn to connect to your inner power, it will shine from your soul through your physical body and into the world. People may say you have a glow about you, or that you seem different or happier. All of the power you need is already within you.

Chapter Nine

GOOD ACTIONS

What are good actions? It means doing something that benefits someone else without expecting anything in return. Good actions may or may not inspire those that you help to do the same for someone else. If they decide to do something nice for someone else and pay it forward because of the nice thing you did for them, then that's awesome, but shouldn't be expected.

You may ask yourself why you should help someone else if there's nothing in it for you. If you're not getting paid, not getting a barter exchange or some other type of benefit, then there's really no reason to get involved, right? While some people might think this way, I disagree. There are plenty of reasons to get involved. What you put out into the Universe comes back to you so why not put out as much good as you can? A good deed is always positive and rewarding within you at a soul level. Sometimes we forget our spiritual roots, our beginnings in the spiritual realm. I call this a *lack of remembrance*. When we remember, and are connected to our spiritual selves, we tend to act with more kindness and gratitude towards others. When we're in a *lack of remembrance* mode, we may be short-tempered, unkind, or mean spirited. To live in spiritual coziness, means to live in warmth and kindness. It's essential that we remember our inner truth, our spiritual self, and treat others the way we want to be treated, with love, respect, and kindness.

When we're genuine in the good actions we take, then the positive energy of those actions has an overflowing effect. It flows from us to other people and from then to even more people. It's like a river flowing over a dam, spreading further and further downstream and positively affecting the people around it.

Unfortunately, in today's world, harboring feelings of criticism, unkindness, or being judgmental seems to be all the rage. But that's not how our souls are made nor is it the way we would act if we were on the spiritual plane. If you're feeling more negative emotions than positive ones, then stop for a minute and consider if you've let the negative situations you've experienced on the earthly plane pull you further away from your spiritual self. If you have, then now is the time to find your way back to center, back to your true essence and reconnect with your soul frequency. Unkindness can't be part of your being when you're living in tune with your spirituality and within the positivity and coziness of good actions. Positive energy flows from the spiritual plane through our bodies and it's just waiting to be released. Be aware when negativity is blocking your positive flow and take steps to turn it around.

Good actions help us to make the best out of any situation. When we are aware of the people in our surroundings, we can choose to be helpful in both small and big ways. Going out of our way to create good actions for others is meaningful and can bring feelings of surprise, happiness, and joy to another person. These are qualities of coziness as well. I choose to spread good actions whenever I can. It makes me feel good inside and to me, knowing that I've been able to help someone in even a very small way, well, that's more important than any monetary gain.

Chapter Nine

Try It Now Exercise:
LETTING GO TO EMBRACE COZINESS

As you're creating coziness for deeper meaning in your life, you'll often discover during the process that you have to let some things go in order to attain an orderly, simpler life. This is an easy exercise to do to let things go.

First, I'd like for you to get an empty box and take it to the middle of a room. You're going to store this box for a while and eventually give it away, so make sure you don't really want to keep anything you put into it. I advise to leave things with sentimental value out of the box because those are things you'll always want to hold on to.

As you're standing there with your box, look around and decide if there is anything that you can let go of that should go inside. Are there decorations that you're tired of looking at? Pictures? Knickknacks that are just sitting there collecting dust? You can do what I call a wall check by looking at one wall then the next and so on. Once you've finished with your walls, then you're going to go into drawers and cabinets.

Sorting through things in your cabinets or drawers can take some time. If clothing items have holes in them, toss them in a trash bag. If containers are half filled with something that you no longer use, or are expired, throw them away too. Clearing out the old will add to your sense of coziness because you're also getting rid of an accumulation of things that are serving no purpose. That being said, you may come across items that you've forgotten you had but you love, which will increase the sense of coziness in your home. Once you've gone through every room of your house then take your box(es) and put them somewhere out of sight—like in an empty room or closet. After a few months have passed, if you haven't had to go back into them for anything then those items can safely be tossed or donated.

You may also find that you have to let go of some of your ways of thinking about how you live in order to settle into a cozy lifestyle. If papers, magazines, or advertisements that come in the mail tend to accumulate, then you'll have to make up your mind to let go of all of those pieces of paper as soon as they arrive to get rid of the clutter they make. If you always feel the need to be with other people, try spending some time alone to feel the coziness within you that only happens when you're by yourself. You may also have to decide that people who aren't supportive or a good influence on you should hit the road. If that's the case, there's a reason you're feeling that way and it is important to listen to your intuition.

Letting go helps you embrace coziness because it allows you to live in a simple, comfortable manner without a lot of distractions, drama, and problems. Letting go of things that keep you from coziness is the quickest way to bring the cozy factor back into your life. It is simplifying everything to transform yourself.

MAKE YOUR OWN MIRACLES

What is a miracle? It is an unexplainable, surprising, transformational event that produces wondrous results. It is the work of God and the Divine on the earthly plane. Every person on this planet is a miracle because we chose to come to this realm and interact with one another to learn specific lessons for spiritual growth. Every day that we live, we create miracles in our own life. Most are small but some are so

Chapter Nine

monumental that they stop us in our tracks. Think of the last time you experienced a miracle in your life. Something that happened to make you feel blessed and filled with gratitude.

What if you could create miracles every day? Miracles can occur naturally when you change your perspective, when you experience revelations regarding your spiritual nature or inner truth, and when you receive an unexpected gift from the Universe. Being who you are within your soul and doing the things that feel right for you is a starting point for creating miracles. From birth, your life is a mission to discover your essential self and soul path, and to grow on that path. Being able to create miracles in your life means you're on the right pathway and you've aligned with your soul purpose, your reason for being.

Let's look at some of the ways you can create miracles in your life. Following your dreams can bring miraculous results. It doesn't matter what the dream is, whether it's big or small. If you strive to achieve your dreams, miracles can unexpectedly happen and open doors for you. I believe that if you're working hard, the Universe rewards that hard work with opportunities, which can be miraculous.

Belief in yourself is important in creating miracles in your life. When you believe you can do something *you will*. If you don't believe you can do something then that can be a self-fulfilling prophecy. Always believe in yourself at a soul level, as a being of energy and light, which has unbounded miracles within that can come to fruition on the earthly plane of existence.

Miracles occur when you take action based on your beliefs. You can hope you get lucky and wait around until something positive occurs but if you discover the steps needed to ensure that what you want happens, then you're taking positive action toward creating that miracle for yourself. It's important to be aware of what is happening in your life so you recognize the miracles when they happen. If you're not aware, the miracle may pass you by simply because you didn't recognize that it was for you.

Instead of limiting yourself by being too specific regarding how your miracle will appear, be open to it appearing any way it wants too. This is when awareness becomes so important. You may think you have to win the lottery to get extra money but what if you started putting coins in a big jug? Before you know it you'll have a lot of money saved without even realizing it. Coins can add up quickly. When you count it out, you may feel like it's a miracle that you've saved so much money simply by saving your coins.

Give yourself permission to create miracles in your life. Then follow a path of awareness by chasing your dreams and having belief in yourself to bring those dreams to fruition.

SPONTANEITY

If you've ever found yourself stuck in a rut, or bored because you're doing the same old thing day after day, that's not very cozy is it? To get yourself moving forward again, and to reconnect to the comfort and soothing feelings of coziness, try adding a little spontaneity to your day. Being spontaneous is when you do something on the spur of the moment, without thinking it out, and without worrying about the outcome of your actions. Spontaneity is when you have an open mind, no worries and feel uninhibited. You do things just to do them.

Chapter Nine

Many people love being spontaneous while others can't stand it. I can respect both sides but I tend to be spontaneous. When I was younger if I wanted to go somewhere I just filled up the car with gas and took off. Now, I can't do that because I have more responsibilities that keep me from going but that doesn't mean I lack spontaneity. Just today, I ended up riding my horse when that definitely wasn't on the agenda since I'm on a tight deadline for this book.

Here's the thing—doing something spontaneous not only lifts your spirits, but it can help you focus better and makes you a more flexible person. It helps you become more disciplined and able to conquer your fears, all while you're changing up your daily routine. Being spontaneous makes you switch gears in your mind. You develop the ability to handle the unexpected, even when you're doing it to yourself by purposefully choosing to be spontaneous. It enables us to handle situations in a relaxed, calm manner. When spontaneity is lacking, it may be more difficult for you to handle changes quickly because you're not used to it. Choosing spontaneity is a positive way to feel more comfortable and cozy with changes with they occur.

So what are some ways that you can add more spontaneity to your day? You can start with little things like choosing a different flavor of toothpaste or eating something different than your normal breakfast. Maybe skip the coffee and have orange juice one morning or really switch it up and have a soda. Being spontaneous means that you can do whatever you want in a responsible manner. If you want to have an extra piece of pie, or cut your long hair short, or dye your hair neon purple then go for it. This is your life to live and if you're having a great time, learning lessons, not hurting anyone, and enjoying the exhilaration that spontaneity gives you—well there's absolutely nothing wrong with that.

When you stop doubting your ability to be spontaneous then you'll discover that it can be more invigorating than you thought possible. It's fun to do something that's completely unexpected. It triggers something in our internal wiring that enables us to make a deep connection within our spiritual selves, so that not only are we doing the unexpected in the physical, we're experiencing the benefits of those actions in our spirituality.

Busyness vs Restfulness

Today people are busier than ever before. There is so much to do and only twenty-four hours to get it all done. Our jobs often take a lot of time, sometimes so much that we have to bring work home with us just to get it all completed on time. If you have kids then you may have events to get them to, school work to help with, and after school activities that take up additional time. If you're so busy that you have little time left for yourself, sometimes it can become emotionally overwhelming and that's not good for you or for those around you. In order to find balance, and avoid coming apart at the seams, you must find time to rest.

On the other hand, if you find yourself with too much time on your hands with nothing to do, you may experience boredom, which can also lead to frustration, anxiety and taking it out on those close to you. You just need to find something to eliminate the boredom and frustration that is caused by having nothing to do. You can start by adding little things to your

Chapter Nine

agenda or jumping head first into a new project. When you can't settle and feel comfortable with yourself, even if you have nothing to do, then boredom is the problem. Boredom arises out of a need to constantly be doing something. If you're always feeling restless, on edge, or out of sorts when you're alone and it's quiet, then it's time to reconnect with your inner self and learn that it's okay to be alone with nothing to do. Being happy with yourself, understanding that you don't have to be super busy or feeling that you have to be doing something with someone else to be happy is the first step in eliminating boredom for good.

Finding the balance between busyness and restfulness is necessary to live a cozy life and once you accomplish it, will transform your life. You can't feel coziness if you're always on the go, if you're frustrated because you're bored, or you're getting too much rest or have nothing to do. But where is that happy medium? Only you can decide what the balance between the two feels like for you. Each of us is different with unique needs. For someone who is accustomed to doing many things in a day, then a few hours of rest at the end of the day may be all you need. Others may need more rest to feel at their optimum best and less busyness. If you begin to feel frazzled, then that's a sign that you're out of balance and need to rest. Or, if you're sleep is being interrupted and you find yourself waking up too much at night, then think about what caused it. For example, last night I ate something too spicy for me and starting around 2:30 in the morning I woke up every twenty to thirty minutes and when I was asleep, I had nightmares. Since I wasn't able to sleep well, today I've been feeling very overwhelmed, even though I'm accustomed to working a lot and getting a lot done in a day. So today, I'm knocking off work early to try to relax some before bedtime in the hopes of getting a solid night's sleep and I'm not eating anything spicy tonight. Take some time to evaluate how busy you are and how much rest you're getting. Figure out a way to balance the two so that you feel upbeat and positive each day. Only do what you can handle without getting overburdened and burned out.

PUT A SPRING IN YOUR STEP

Walking with a spring in your step means that you are moving in an energetic way that depicts a happy, confident, and positive mood. It also indicates a spiritual coziness within you. The way you move your physical body can have an effect on your mind, body, and spirit connection so it's important to be aware of the way you're carrying yourself.

As humans, walking is an essential part of our makeup. While we now have cars to take us places, we still have to walk to the car. Walking is an excellent way to get exercise and reconnect with nature. If you don't currently have a walking plan in place, that's totally fine. This section will help you even if you're just walking around the grocery store.

So exactly how do you put a spring in your step? First become aware of how you're walking. Are you looking ahead or looking down at your feet? Are you picking up your feet then slapping them flat on the ground or are you bouncing along on the balls of your feet, or maybe you're dragging your feet? Is your body hunched forward or is your spine straight? Ideally, you should be looking forward, back and body straight, arms swinging naturally by your side, a medium sized stride, and there should be a very slight bounce in your step. This bounce

Chapter Nine

is the spring in your step. To understand what it feels like, stand on the balls of your feet, then lower your heels up and down in quick succession. You'll feel the muscles in your calf working with this effort. A slight bounce is all it takes, you don't need to look like you're jumping on a pogo stick while you're walking—that's taking it too far. You'll keep your stride to a medium length because it's easy to lose the bounce if you're taking huge strides.

Adding a spring to your step helps tremendously during a walk because it's a better overall workout but there are more benefits too. A spring in your step helps build your confidence. So if you're unsure about something that you have to do, give yourself a little pep talk and add that spring to your step and you'll come across as confident and assured to those around you. A spring in your step can change a bad mood into a good one. If you're feeling out of sorts, make yourself get outside and go for a walk with a spring in your step. Before you know it, you might just be whistling a tune or humming a song as you walk.

The light, carefree feeling of happiness often translates to a spring in your step without you even realizing it. Have you ever seen someone walking along with a little bounce to their step and thought, *that person sure is happy*? Seeing someone else with a spring in their step often rubs off on us and raises our frequency, and then, before we know it, we're walking down the sidewalk with a spring in our step too.

Cozy living is all about being happy, feeling warmth, and putting a spring in your step helps you connect to happiness and the coziness of life. If you don't have time for a walk, just trying bouncing in place while imagining yourself feeling happy, carefree, and confident. You don't have to actually go somewhere to reap similar benefits of taking a long leisurely stroll through the park. You can bounce on the balls of your feet for ten minutes while you're cooking dinner. It's a great stress reliever too.

YOUR VALUES AND BELIEFS

Your values and beliefs are key components to living a cozy life filled with purpose, meaning, and direction. It is more than *what* you do, more than the daily grind of working to pay bills. It is *who* you are as a spiritual being and how you let your light shine into the world that matters most. If your morals, values, and beliefs aren't clear to you from a spiritually universal perspective, then you can get off track and out of balance, maybe stuck in a rut without forward motion, which makes it harder to settle into the comfort and coziness of a life filled with joy and happiness.

Values are the principles that you live by. They are the motor behind your behaviors, the things you say and do. They are what determine your thoughts on different situations, world views, and the expectations you place upon yourself and others. Values are the things that are important to you. If you're a person that values honesty and integrity then you're not going to lie and cheat, or have friends that participate in dishonest practices, or who are unreliable. Values affect your beliefs. You may believe that a person's word is their bond, but then you find out they're being dishonest with you, which affects your thoughts and feelings regarding that person and how you chose to interact with them in the future.

Chapter Nine

When you view life from a universal perspective you are very aware of your own spirituality, your core essence, and the path you're chosen to live. You're also very aware of others as spiritual beings. You realize that they've chosen their own path which may be very different from yours. It's seeing that each person's journey is one of self-discovery, of learning who they are on a soul level, and being open-minded to the journey of others. It's understanding that we are all part of something bigger than ourselves, part of the universal scheme, and each one of us have our own unique place within that plan. Thinking this way allows us to see each other's differences and a greater understanding within ourself, which may affect or change our own personal values and belief system.

As we progress along our spiritual path our experiences affect our values and beliefs. When you personally experience something that you never thought was possible then your point of view changes. Nonbelievers become believers. I never believed in ghosts until I had one squeeze my shoulder from behind, when I was sitting with my back against a wall. That first experience forever changed my belief about ghosts. Once your belief has been changed, it's not your place to force what you now believe on someone else. Value and belief systems are as unique and individual as each of our souls. When the time is right, the teacher will come.

Evaluating your values and beliefs from time to time is important to your soul growth and prevents you from getting stuck in a rut. When you evaluate your values and beliefs at a universal level, then you can find new ways to implement them into your life. You can also help others learn to connect with their own inner source, their sense of values and beliefs, and find a connection to the spiritual. Values and beliefs are for each of us individually, but they are also for the collective consciousness of us all.

Your Soul Journey Frequency

Just as every person, animal and place has its own unique frequency, the path you chose to walk in this lifetime has a unique frequency too. Your *soul journey frequency* is the way your energy fluctuates as you move along your life path. It is directly affected by your spiritual frequency. It is usually in forward motion but can get clogged up so that it's moving slower than normal or cleared so that it moves faster than normal.

Your soul journey frequency can be different than your spiritual frequency during times of change. If you find yourself taking the wrong path, your soul journey frequency may increase to try to urge you to the correct pathway. It can also help steer you in the right direction when you're going the wrong way.

Let's take a look at some of the things that can affect your soul journey frequency. When you're learning new information, discovering more about your own spirituality you're zooming along your frequency highway because discovery causes an increase in your personal frequency. During times when your personal frequency is slower because of illness or being overwhelmed, then your soul journey frequency will slow down too. But what about times when you're facing a situation where you have choices to make and you're unsure what to do? What if you make the wrong choice? Your soul journey frequency may speed up or slow down and

Chapter Nine

be in direct contradiction with your personal frequency. You may be trying to hurry up and get things done when in fact you need to slow down for some reason. In a case like this you may experience stumbling blocks on your path, things that are slowing you down when you don't want to slow down. This is your soul journey frequency helping you out and trying to get you into balance. There's a reason that you need to slow down even if you don't know it yet. On the other hand, when you should be moving faster than you actually are, everything you touch seems to work quickly and easily. This is your soul journey frequency speeding you up.

We have each determined a specific number of lessons to learn in this lifetime. Once we move from our spiritual form to our human form it's easy to forget what we've set out to do. The soul journey frequency is a way to help keep us on track, to help us realize our own spiritual energy, our sense of spiritual coziness, and to allow them to work together so we can reach our fullest spiritual potential during our time on the earthly plane of existence. The more you strengthen your connection to the spiritual realm, to your inner core essence, to your spiritual frequency, your soul journey frequency, and the universe, the more you'll learn. Becoming aware of the soul journey frequency also helps you to live a cozier life. When you feel the energy change, then you'll know instinctively when you should slow down, experience, and appreciate the little, cozy things that settle and bring balance to your soul.

If you're not at this point yet, look for areas of your life where you can make improvements, where you can connect to the frequency of your journey, understand the depth of your soul, and the growth that is available to you if you'll only look for it. Recognize it and implement it into your life. The journey is filled with challenges but the energy surrounding you along the way will guide and protect you.

THE UNIVERSAL COZY CONNECTION

There is a connection between cozy living and understanding the relationship we have as spiritual beings within the Universe. Energy flows throughout the Universe, creating positive and negatives, causing change and creation. Once we are aware of this energy flow, we can use it with purpose to create positive changes in our life, to raise our frequency to higher levels, and to become one with our spiritual selves. It is a key to transformation.

When you're connected to the energy of spiritual coziness it helps you to better see and understand these connections to the Universe and the Divine. You'll tend to take quick actions when you're struck with inspirational ideas that are true to your spiritual essence. In turn, your action can help others through your creations. Let's say you are an artist that creates beautiful inspirational paintings. One day you're contemplating your connection to the Universe and see in your mind's eye an image that you transfer onto canvas. When others see this painting they tell you what they get from it and how it makes them feel. You realize that this image is helping others understand their spiritual nature better. Or maybe you teach others about their intuition and one day you receive a message that really hits home with your spirituality. You share that message with others through your teachings and it helps them to gain more Universal knowledge.

Chapter Nine

The Universal stream of consciousness is filled with unlimited knowledge that is yours for the taking. Ideas are plentiful and one may be specific to your spiritual or personal growth on the earthly plane of existence. Coziness gives you clarity of mind so that it is easier for you to comprehend ideals that may seem foreign to you at first. Take what fits and make it your own, and if it's still unclear it may be meant for you to understand at a later date. If it is, it will come back around to you again in the future and, at that time, may make perfect sense to you.

On a spiritual level, our connection with the spiritual realm and the Universe helps us to understand our purpose here on the earthly plane. It makes us dig deeper to learn as much as we can about why we chose to incarnate in the first place. Your purpose may be that of a caregiver, teacher, leader, follower, inventor, or artist just to name a few. Once you have determined your overall purpose you can define it even further. Our purpose in life often deals with helping others either directly or indirectly and can manifest as gifts that we share with others or challenges that we help others meet. Whatever your purpose, you can gain clarity through coziness.

I like to take a few minutes every day to purposefully make a connection to my spiritual essence and the Universe just to see if there's anything new going on, if I have a message from my higher self, or just to contemplate my path. I'll often receive information that I wasn't expecting about things that I need to do to make things right on my path. Usually, it has to do with spiritual growth or getting back in balance because I tend to do too much all of the time. By taking these few minutes to get cozy and just contemplate my path at a Universal level, it helps to keep me in forward motion. It you have some free time during the day it's a great way to learn more about yourself through the Universal cozy connection.

Try It Now Exercise:
COZINESS TRANSFORMATIONAL CHALLENGE

Are you ready to add more coziness into your life? To find a deeper connection to your inner self? To feel more warmth, love, serenity, and joy in your life? Now that you know all of the ways you can grow through the spirituality of coziness, it's time to implement these changes in your life. It's time to participate in your own Coziness Transformational Challenge.

The first thing you need to do is to set a specific start date for your program. This is going to be your point of activation. This is the date you've chosen to actively make changes in your life to add more coziness to it. The program you'll follow for your Coziness Transformational Challenge is within the pages of this book. Define the areas you would like to improve upon, study that section of the book, and follow the examples or exercises.

The hardest part of any transformational challenge is choosing to begin and then sticking with it. If you've ever started an exercise or weight-loss program it's a similar process. You have to be aware of the choices you're making along the way and you have to care about, and want to achieve, the end results. When you activate your internal sense of coziness, the end result is more awareness, changes within your home, and changes within your thought patterns and spirituality. This adds more positivity to your emotional, physical, and spiritual health for your mind, body, and spirit.

Chapter Nine

To have the most success, make sure you're ready and willing to accept the changes you'll make in your life. Then set your start date. The time has to be right for you to achieve the most success and you'll instinctively feel when it's right. As you practice, adding coziness to your life will become effortless. It will be a seamless flow brimming over with positivity.

The best way to keep up with your progress is to keep a journal specifically for this exercise. You can even write Coziness Transformational Challenge right across the front and glue pictures to the front of it like you would on a vision board, which will make it all the more cozy itself. Any time you have a cozy event write down what you did, how it was received by others, and what you could do differently next time to make it even cozier. Write down ways you implemented a feeling of coziness to your personal life each day. Also refer back to the practices list after the table of contents to see if there are any you haven't tried yet or you'd like to do again. Write how you felt about the change and whether you feel like it worked or not.

You can do the Coziness Transformational Challenge for as short or as long of a time as you like. There's isn't an end date to finish. This is a life change, so take as long as you need to make it. You might try for thirty days to start with and make a point to practice every day. After that you could choose to take a break and do the challenge again at another time or you might decide that it's working so well you want to keep going. It's all up to you. This is a choice to add warmth and coziness to your life so make sure you're having fun and enjoying every minute of it.

Conclusion

Leading a cozy life truly is simple. It takes an effort to begin but once you're on the path, it becomes second nature. I've introduced you to many different ways that you can add coziness to all aspects of your life. When you think of coziness, it's more than just sitting by a warm fire drinking cocoa. It expands into all parts of your life including your home, family, friends, your emotional and spiritual coziness, and finding coziness in nature. Along the way, you've read how to connect with the energy and the frequency of coziness and how to use it to raise your frequency and the frequencies of others that you're in contact with.

We are always growing and changing, learning more on a spiritual level and about our existence on the earthly plane. If you try to grow a little each day by learning new ways to bring coziness into your life, then you're practicing spiritual cozy living. Challenge yourself daily. Make different choices. Spend time with family and friends. Take time to immerse yourself in nature. Create places where you feel peaceful and filled with love. That's living a cozy life.

My wish for you is all the growth you can achieve through cozy living, through having an open mind, and challenging yourself to be the best, strongest, and most successful spiritual being you can be in this lifetime. Have fun and enjoy yourself as you learn the lessons you choose for yourself. Some may be difficult, others easy, but if you surround yourself with the energy of coziness they'll all benefit your soul's growth.

Conclusion

I hope this book has been helpful and guided you along the path as you seek to create more coziness in your life. I appreciate that you took time out of your busy day to read my words.

BIBLIOGRAPHY

Alvarez, Melissa. *Animal Frequency: What Are Your Power Animal Spirit Guides Trying to Tell You? Identify, Attune, and Connect to the Energy of Animals.* Adrema Press, 2023.

Breathnach, Sarah Ban. *The Simple Abundance Companion: Following Your Authentic Path to Something More* . New York: Warner Books, 2000.

DeMoss, Nancy Leigh. *Choosing Gratitude: Your Journey to Joy.* Chicago, IL: Moody Publishers, 2009.

Dunne, Linnea. Lagom: *The Swedish Art of Balanced Living.* New York: Gaia Books, 2017.

Gump, Andrew. *Daily Routine: What Makes the Difference between Highly Successful People and Unsuccessful People—Become the Master of your Life.* Self-published on Amazon Digital Services, 2017.

Gunaratana, Bhante Henepola. *The Four Foundations of Mindfulness in Plain English.* Somerville, MA: Wisdom Publications, 2012.
———. *Mindfulness in Plain English.* Somerville, MA: Wisdom Publications, 2011.

Henderson, Emily. *Styled: Secrets for Arranging Rooms, from Tabletops to Bookshelves.* New York: Potter Style, 2015.

Bibliography

Holm, Emily. *Hygge Danish Life: The Art of Living Joyful, Hygge, and Clutter-Free Lives.* Self-published on Amazon Digital Services, 2016.

Johansen, Signe. *How to Hygge: The Nordic Secrets to a Happy Life.* New York: St. Martin's Press, 2017.

Kabat-Zinn, Jon. *Wherever You Go, There You Are: Mindfulness Meditation In Everyday Life.* New York: Hachette Book Group, Hyperion eBook, 2009.

Martin, Cory. *Yoga for Beginners: Simple Yoga Poses to Calm Your Mind and Strengthen Your Body.* Berkeley, CA: Rockridge Press, 2015.

Morin, Amy. *13 Things Mentally Strong People Don't Do: Take Back Your Power, Embrace Change, Face Your Fears, and Train Your Brain for Happiness and Success.* New York: Harper Collins, 2014.

Prochaska, James O., John Norcross, and Carlo DiClemente. *Changing for Good: A Revolutionary Six-Stage Program for Overcoming Bad Habits and Moving Your Life Positively Forward.* New York: William Morrow and Company/Avon Books, 1994.

Radjou, Navi, Jaideep Prabhu, and Simone Ahuja. *Jugaad Innovation: Think Frugal, Be Flexible, Generate Breakthrough Growth.* Hoboken, NJ: Jossey-Bass, 2012.

Santos, Brian. *Faux Finish Secrets: From Brian Santos the Wall Wizard.* Des Moines, IA: Merideth Publishing Group, 2006.

Stein, Diane. *Essential Reiki: A Complete Guide to an Ancient Healing Art.* New York: Crossing Press, 1995.

Sunim, Haemin. *The Things You Can See Only When You Slow Down: How to Be Calm and Mindful in a Fast-Paced World.* New York: Penguin Books, 2012.

Tolle, Eckhart. *The Power of Now: A Guide to Spiritual Enlightenment.* Novato, CA and Vancouver, BC, Canada: Namaste Publishing and New World Library, 2010.

Webster's New World™ Dictionary and Thesaurus, Second Edition, New York: Hungry Minds, 2002.

Young, Janet. *The Subconscious Mind and Its Illuminating Light: An Interpretation.* San Francisco, CA: 1909.

WEBSITES

Bostwick, Leah M. / Sun Signs, *Symbolic Meaning of Seasons,* http://www.sunsigns.org/symbolic-meaning-of-seasons/

Brones, Anna / Kitchn, *What Is Fika? An Introduction to the Swedish Coffee Break,* http://www.thekitchn.com/what-in-the-world-is-fika-an-intro-to-the-swedish-coffee-break-the-art-of-fika-219297

Bibliography

Frater, Jaime / Listverse, *10 Words That Can't Be Translated to English*, http://listverse.com/2010/09/23/10-words-that-cant-be-translated-to-english/

Gallagher, Sophie / Huffington Post UK, *Lagom Is the Swedish Trend Everyone Will Be Following In 2017, Here's How to Do It*, http://www.huffingtonpost.co.uk/entry/lagom-swedish-lifestyle-trend_uk_586d00dfe4b0d590e4501724

Giovanni / Live and Dare, *Types of Meditation: An Overview of 23 Meditation Techniques*, http://liveanddare.com/types-of-meditation/

Goldhill, Olivia / Quartz, *The Untranslatable Scandinavian Words for Coziness Describe a Very Particular Winter Joy*, https://qz.com/601561/scandinavians-untranslatable-word-for-winter-coziness-might-explain-why-theyre-they-happiest-people-on-earth/

Gunaratana, Bhante Henepola / Lion's Roar, *Living with Awareness: Introducing the Four Foundations of Mindfulness*, https://www.lionsroar.com/living-with-awareness-an-excerpt-from-the-four-foundations-of-mindfulness-in-plain-english/

Hart, Anna / The Telegraph, *Goodbye Hygge, Hello Lagom: The Secret of Swedish Contentment*, http://www.telegraph.co.uk/wellbeing/mood-and-mind/goodbye-hygge-hello-lagom-secret-swedish-contentment/

Roberts, Gretchen / Whole Living, *Wabi-Sabi Your Life: 6 Strategies for Embracing Imperfection*, http://www.wholeliving.com/133628/wabi-sabi-your-life-6-strategies-embracing-imperfection

Vartan, Starre / Mother Nature Network, *7 Cultural Concepts We Don't Have in the U.S.*, http://www.mnn.com/lifestyle/arts-culture/blogs/7-cultural-concepts-we-dont-have-in-the-us

Venefica, Avia / Dare to Discern What's Your Sign, *Symbolic Meaning of Seasons*, http://www.whats-your-sign.com/symbolic-meaning-of-seasons.html

Wallace, Scott / National Geographic, *Exclusive: Stunning New Photos of Isolated Tribe Yield Surprises*, http://news.nationalgeographic.com/2016/12/uncontacted-tribe-amazon-brazil-photos/

Walsh, Carla / Fitness Magazine, *Find Your Fit: The 5 Most Popular Yoga Styles*, http://www.fitnessmagazine.com/workout/yoga/help/yoga-class-styles/

Woolsey, Barbara / Thrillist, *How Norwegians Stay Happy During Long, Brutal Winters*, https://www.thrillist.com/lifestyle/nation/a-guide-to-koselig-the-norwegian-concept-that-helps-prevent-wintertime-depression

www.ingramcontent.com/pod-product-compliance
Lightning Source LLC
Chambersburg PA
CBHW062048080426
42734CB00012B/2583